In memory of my grandfather

JOHN C. PURVES,

co-inventor of the autopilot for planes.

He wants to turn you on to

the world of invention and patents.

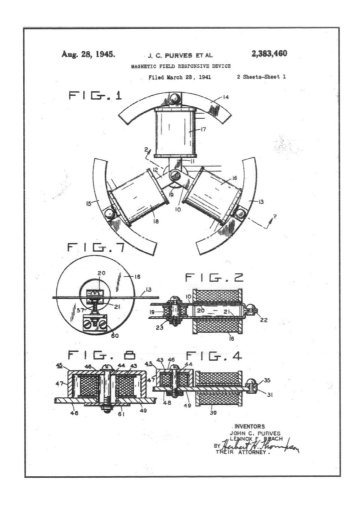

A NOTE TO READERS AND THEIR PARENTS

Some of the projects in this book require the use
of sharp objects or power tools. Those projects include:

- Handmade Paper
- Paper Snowflake
- Crystal Snowflake
- Kaleidoscope
- Water Bomb
- Jumping Jack
- Simple Wishing Well
- Puppet Theater and Curtain
- Small Corral with Self-Closing Gate
- Violin Plant Stand
- Homemade Stilts
- Sailboat
- Marionette
- My Childhood Bird Kite
- Kite
- Simple Helicopter
- Parachute
- Ames Trapezoidal Window
- Stereoscope
- Ames Illusion Room
- Solar System Diorama

As you and your kids work on these projects
and use these tools, please ensure that you do so safely.

We have flagged the projects that require any sharp objects or power
tools with the below symbol, so you can keep an eye out for it as you go.

VISUALIZING, UNDERSTANDING, CREATING

I used to ask my grandfather science questions all the time like *Why is the sky blue?* and *Why is grass green?* Most parents usually don't know or have forgotten the answers to questions like that, but my grandfather was an engineer and inventor, and he would explain that the Earth's atmosphere has an effect on the sun's color spectrum, which is why the sky is blue. As he explained this, I visualized a picture that my elementary school teacher had shown us of the solar system. We had learned that the Earth's atmosphere is very thin. If the Earth were an apple, the atmosphere would be its skin. While thinking about this, I visualized a childhood picnic I was at when I saw a smokestack making a swirl of dirty black smoke against a blue sky. I asked several adults if the smoke would make the air darker and dirty. I was told that it just disappears, but I did not believe it. I could visualize the atmosphere as being thin like the skin of an apple, and I knew the dirty smoke would get trapped beneath it.

Ever since I was young, I connected words with pictures, which is why I can easily translate abstract ideas into detailed drawings like the ones I made for engineering projects. The first books your parents read to you probably connected pictures to words. Learning the word for the image was the point: apple, ball, cat, and so forth. In school, we are also taught to learn with words first. But for me, words were always less important. If I can picture something, I can understand it. And then I can create it.

OTHER BOOKS YOU MAY ENJOY

CALLING ALL MINDS

TEMPLE GRANDIN

With Betsy Lerner

PUFFIN BOOKS

PUFFIN BOOKS
An imprint of Penguin Random House LLC, New York

First published in the United States of America by Philomel Books,
an imprint of Penguin Random House LLC, 2018
Published by Puffin Books, an imprint of Penguin Random House LLC, 2019

Visit us online at penguinrandomhouse.com

THE LIBRARY OF CONGRESS HAS CATALOGED THE PHILOMEL BOOKS EDITION AS FOLLOWS:
Names: Grandin, Temple, author.
Title: Calling all minds / Temple Grandin.
Description: New York, NY : Philomel Books, [2018] | "Philomel Books, an imprint of Penguin Random
House LLC." | Audience: Ages 8–12. | Audience: Grades 4 to 6. | Includes bibliographical references.
Identifiers: LCCN 2017027602 | ISBN 9781524738204 (hardcover) | ISBN 9781524738211 (e-book)
Subjects: LCSH: Science—Experiments—Juvenile literature. | Inventions—Juvenile literature. |
Handicraft—Juvenile literature.
Classification: LCC Q164 .G67 2018 | DDC 507.8—dc23
LC record available at https://lccn.loc.gov/2017027602

Puffin Books ISBN 9781524738228

Printed in the United States of America.

7th Printing

Edited by Jill Santopolo and Talia Benamy.
Design by Ellice M. Lee.
Text set in Granjon Lt Std.

CONTENTS

INTRODUCTION

My road to becoming an inventor and animal scientist began when I was young. I attended my classes, but I was more interested in the horses than anything else. I was lucky because both my mother and the school's headmaster encouraged me to learn everything I could about animals and science, and my teachers allowed it as long as I was on time for classes and meals and took care of the horses. In addition to riding, that meant grooming, feeding, and mucking out the stalls. Summers at my aunt's ranch were also extremely important; I spent all my time with the cattle and horses learning everything I could about their behavior and how to communicate with them. Another influence was John C. Purves, my maternal grandfather. He was an inventor and one of the great role models in my life. When I was a child, I asked him endless

Me in high school

questions about the world around, such as *Why do the tides on the seashore go in and out?*

Another reason I became a scientist, which I didn't figure out until I was older, is that I'm a visual thinker. I organize the world through pictures, and my mind references words through series of visual images. If someone says "dog," my mind calls up each dog I have ever seen. As I got older, I could picture how things worked in vivid visual detail and in three dimensions. It was like running a film in my head. Eventually, I could actually test run equipment in my imagination. I could see things *that* clearly. It's considered "normal" to use a combination of visual and verbal skills to express thoughts and ideas, but in my experience there is no "normal."

When I was diagnosed with autism (as a child in the 1950s), most people didn't really know what it was or the different ways it affected people. Now, we say that a person is "on the autistic spectrum," which can mean many things. They may have normal speech, or they may never learn to speak at all. I was a late talker, I hated being hugged or held, and I was often in my own world. I had so much difficulty sitting still that Mother used to say to me, "Go outside and run the energy out of you!" I also couldn't stand sudden sounds or any clothes that were too scratchy, and I would become very agitated when my world was changed in any little way. Others rock back and forth all the time or need to spin themselves around and can't pay attention. Many can be socially awkward and unable to make eye contact, yet can have successful careers in tech companies, industrial design, the arts, or a job that requires attention to detail. Some develop special skills at a very advanced level, often in the areas of mathematics, art, computers, or music. Some great scientists and inventors were probably on the autism spectrum.

Autism is not "one size fits all." The more we learn about "the spectrum" (the range of abilities and deficits an autistic person may have), the more we will understand different kinds of minds and how important different kinds of thinkers are—especially where creativity, innovation, and invention are concerned. I like to think of myself and other people who are different kinds of thinkers on a human spectrum. Though our brains may work in different ways, there is no limit to the kinds of contributions we can make.

I got teased a lot in school because my social skills weren't all that great. I knew I didn't fit in, but I didn't know why. The kids called me "tape recorder" because I repeated things over and over in a kind of monotone voice. I cared more about working on science projects and making fancy horse bridles than about the high school dance. Kids still get teased today for differences. Today, I would probably be called a nerd or a geek. Though it's also true that nerds and geeks tend to win Nobel Prizes and run Silicon Valley.

Teachers and parents worry about the quirky kid who draws all day or the one who cares only about insects. They want kids to be well-rounded, but those single-minded kids may grow up to create and do incredible things if we encourage them to pursue their interests. At least that's what happened with me. My love of horses and cattle as a teen became the basis of my career as an animal scientist. No question. However, the main reason I also became an inventor is simple: Ever since I was a child, I've always loved making things and working with my hands. If one of my projects failed, I would experiment for many hours until I got it to work.

When I was young, my mother let me use every kind of material from around the house to create my experiments, from her old clothes and scarves to the cardboard inside my father's shirts when they came back from the cleaners. That cardboard was treasure! I could make a million things with it: building blocks that became forts, dioramas, models, and jumping jacks. I loved taking things apart and putting them back together, or making new inventions out of the pieces. You'll find lots of these projects in this book, but I also encourage you to experiment and design your own. Remember: instructions are only guidelines. Sometimes my students will come to me very upset because they followed the directions to an experiment perfectly, but it didn't produce the desired result. I tell them the same thing: you have to experiment with the experiment!

When my grandfather, who developed the autopilot technology for airplanes, came up with his invention, he had to tinker to make it work. It sensed the direction of the earth's magnetic field, but occasionally it failed. The solution he came up with was to move the device far away from his workshop, which was over a train garage. He realized that the large steel trains moving under his shop had been causing the failures, because their metal was interfering with the device's magnetic sensors. When he moved it away from the steel trains (much like an airplane up in the air would be far away from any disturbances), everything worked as intended.

If I had to boil this book down, my message would be this: Make Things.

I'm sure you've been told by your parents many times to stop playing video games or to get off your iPad or smartphone. They probably say that you are destroying brain cells or that you should be socializing or studying or practicing violin. All of that may be true, but I want you to put down your phone so that one day you might invent a better phone or video game, or a safer car or a piece of equipment that will save lives. For all the amazing things technology can do, if you want to create, you need to take things apart and put them back together with your own hands. Mathematician Dr. Grace Murray Hopper, the inventor of COBOL, the first non-numerical computer code (the one that most humans could understand), famously took apart every alarm clock in her parents' house (seven clocks!) when she was a child. That's usually a sign that a kid is headed for the laboratory; that is, if he or she is encouraged instead of punished for destroying the family clocks.

Grace Murray Hopper at the computer

My father's toolbox was more interesting to me than my mother's jewelry box. They both had little compartments, which I liked to root around in, but the toolbox had all sorts of things I could play with, like adjustable wrenches, drills, and a folding yardstick. The yardstick was made of wood and had many hinges so that when it was closed, it looked like a gate. Partly opened, it looked like a fan, and fully opened, it became a sword to play with. A neighbor had a retractable measuring tape that could be pulled out to twenty-five feet and had a mechanism to lock it at any length. But the part I loved was when you released the catch. The measuring tape went flying back into its body, swallowing itself superfast like the retractable cords on some vacuum cleaners and dog leashes. I've always loved any gadget where rapid movement is involved, so I unscrewed the case and discovered that the measuring tape was connected to a flat metal spring that is wound around a post. That's how all retractable items work.

You need to understand how a car works before you can invent a better one, which means you need to understand how pistons and engines and brake systems work by holding and feeling them. I'm not suggesting you take apart the family car, but if you love cars, you'll learn more by working as a part-time assistant at a local body shop than by playing video games for hours in your family den. You may have to do a lot of sweeping up and menial jobs at first, but eventually you'll get to see under the car and under the hood where the real action is. There is no substitute for real world experience and working with your hands. And there is no greater pride than to see something you have created give pleasure or help people.

▷ ▷ ▷

When the first man landed on the moon, he planted an American flag on its surface to symbolically say "We got here first." When inventors create something, they go to the patent office with their new creation to declare the same thing: "This is a first! This is original!" Patents protect inventors' work by preventing others from stealing both their ideas and often many years of work. The patents themselves tell a remarkable story of human ingenuity and serve a greater public good by preserving knowledge. If you think of a museum as a repository of art, the United States Patent and Trademark Office can be thought of as repository of knowledge. I still love looking up patents to this day. In this book, we'll trace some of the most groundbreaking inventions from Colonial America to the Industrial Age to our present Technological Age. We'll meet the first patent holder, as well as the youngest, the first woman, and the first African American to hold patents. Women and people of color were not originally allowed to hold patents, which is why many of their contributions have been lost to history; their stories are all the more remarkable.

When I was in elementary school, I had a book of inventors that I loved. It's long gone, but I can remember how I read it over and over again until the pages got thin, fascinated by the inventors and the incredible things they made. I remember the entry for Thomas Alva Edison, who held 1,093 patents in the U.S. alone. I was inspired by his saying, "Genius is one percent inspiration and ninety-nine percent perspiration." I was also surprised to learn that

Source: Library of Congress

Thomas Edison

some inventions happen by accident. Early on, I realized three very important things from my book of inventors: (1) There is usually a fascinating story of how things get made by connecting the dots. (2) Inventing takes hard work and requires patience. (3) Sometimes the most important discoveries are the result of serendipity.

The future holds many crucial challenges such as understanding the impact of climate change, curing diseases, and ending hunger. We need all kinds of minds if we are going to figure out how to adapt. If we lose the ability to make things, we will lose a whole lot more. We need people who can cast iron and chemists who can create new materials that are lighter and stronger than metal. We need new storytellers, filmmakers, musicians, and artists. And we need new technologies to explore the future, including a deeper and more complex understanding of the earth and the ocean and the galaxies.

There is no better way to start than by making things of your own design. All the projects I made when I was young contributed to the inventions I've made throughout my life. And they have given my life meaning. I hope these projects and the ones you create will do the same for you.

• CHAPTER ONE •

THINGS MADE OF PAPER

When I was a child, I loved looking at the beautiful patterns snow-flakes made as they landed on my father's car just before they melted and disappeared. I first made paper snowflakes for Christmas decorations in elementary school, taping them to the windows of our classroom. No matter how many snowflakes I made for our school decorations, I always loved that feeling of gently opening the paper and seeing the mirror design. All we needed to make them was paper and scissors.

The word "paper" comes from "papyrus," which was used in ancient Egypt. Papyrus was made of plants and fibers that were soaked in water and then dried and pressed together. For centuries, the same basic method was used. You can still make paper the way the Egyptians did, if you don't mind the coarse surface.

◁ ◁ ◁ **HANDMADE PAPER** ▷ ▷ ▷

These instructions make approximately 5 sheets of paper.

This will be great, messy fun.

You'll need:

- 6 to 10 sheets of construction paper, or any non-shiny paper you find in recycling bins
- Blender
- 2 gallons of warm water, for use in the blender and in the shallow container
- Large, shallow container such as a roasting pan (large enough to accommodate the splatter guards)
- Spoon
- Dried roses and/or herbs, finely chopped
- Dry, clean dish towel
- 2 screen splatter guards (the type used when making bacon—these should be easy to find online)
- Sponge

To create:

1. Tear paper into small pieces (1-inch x 2-inch or 2-inch x 3-inch) and put into the blender. Cover with warm water and let soak for 15 minutes to thoroughly saturate the paper.

2. Pulse the mixture in the blender five to six times until it resembles a thick soup. This is called "paper slurry." If it is too thick, very slowly add a little water. If the slurry is too thin it will yield a paper that will tear or separate.

3. Fill your shallow container with two inches of the warm water. Slowly add the paper slurry to the water and mix with a spoon.

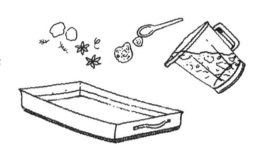

4. At this point you can add chopped dried flowers and/ or herbs as decoration.

5. Spread the dry dish towel out flat on the counter or table.

6. Dip one of your splatter guards into the slurry mixture, making sure the screen is evenly covered. Hold the mixture steady (do not tilt) and place on top of the dish towel. Cover the first splatter guard with the second one.

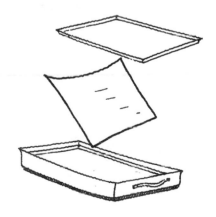

7. Using the sponge, soak up as much water as you can from the top of the second splatter guard.

The more water you can soak up, the shorter the drying time for your handmade paper.

8. Gently remove the top splatter guard. Allow the bottom splatter guard to dry for approximately 6 hours. When thoroughly dry, gently lift the paper from the screen. Hopefully, your paper is ready for use! If your paper is a sticky mess, experiment with different types of paper at the beginning.

IN THE BEGINNING

....

The creation of modern paper and printing began in the fifteenth century when the German printer and inventor

Johannes Gutenburg

Johannes Gutenberg invented movable type. Some historians believe his father was a goldsmith and that Gutenberg grew up around metals and smithing. We will see that a great majority of inventors developed skills at a young age by working closely within their family business or learning a trade. Gutenberg worked in the goldsmiths' guild where he learned the technique of making coins from molds.

These skills led to his invention of type (or letters) made out of metals. He also developed an oil-based ink for the printing process. Until then, books were copied by hand or printed using woodblocks. Both methods were extremely labor intensive and took vast amounts of time.

According to "Gutenberg's Legacy," a study on the impact of moveable type at the Harry Ransom Center's website at the University of Texas at Austin, there were about thirty thousand printed books (made by hand or woodblock) throughout Europe. Fifty years later, with the widespread use of Gutenberg's invention, ten to twelve million books were in circulation. Some estimates put that number at twenty million!

I wonder if Gutenberg could have possibly imagined that his moveable type machine would change the history of printing, or that his invention was largely responsible for the Age of Enlightenment and the Scientific Revolution. Moveable type was like the internet of its time.

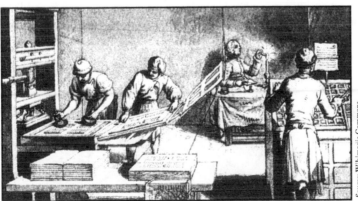

Movable type machine

Source: Wikimedia Commons

How did we get from papyrus to the paper we have all around us? Invention is a process that can happen over one lifetime or over many centuries. That's what interests me: connecting the dots.

A school field trip I still remember was when we visited the local newspaper and watched the papers being printed. They used a Linotype machine to make the metal type. Imagine a typewriter keyboard hooked up to a machine that makes letters from an alloy

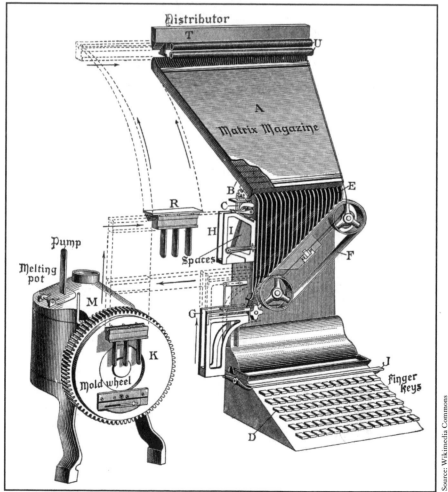

Linotype machine

or mixture of molten lead, tin, and antimony (the same components Gutenberg used). The operator typed our names into the machine, and it produced a warm metallic slab for each of us with our names spelled out in raised letters. Each slab looked like a row of keys from an old-fashioned typewriter. The Linotype machine was invented in the late 1800s by Ottmar Mergenthaler. He is sometimes referred to as the second Gutenberg.

PLEASE DON'T STEREOTYPE ME

Born in Germany in 1854, Ottmar Mergenthaler was an apprentice to a watchmaker and went to a technical school at night. He came to America at eighteen and worked in a cousin's

Source: Wikimedia Commons

Ottmar Mergenthaler

machine shop where he first had the idea of building a machine that would set type automatically. After much trial and error, Mergenthaler saw a way to combine two processes: setting the type (casting) and printing (stamping). On February 10, 1885, he received a patent for "a machine for producing stereotype matrice." A stereotype was the actual metal plate that was used to print multiple copies.

The same word that's commonly used today to describe a certain "stereotype" (the peppy cheerleader, the nerdy scientist) has its roots in Mergenthaler's machine.

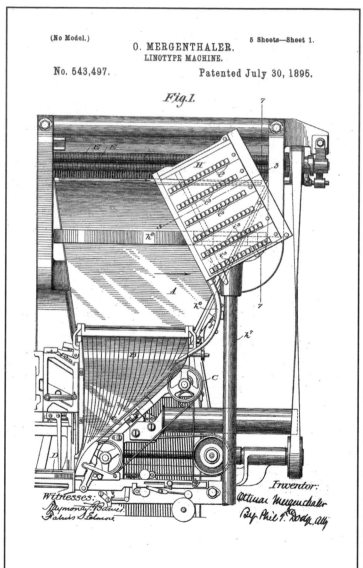

Patent No. US543497A for a Linotype
machine by Ottmar Mergenthaler

Mergenthaler was indebted to Christopher Sholes, along with partners Carlos Glidden and Samuel W. Soulé, who patented the "Type Writer Machine" in 1868, seventeen years before the Linotype. Though numerous inventors had been working on similar machines throughout the 1800s and before, Sholes and his partners were the first to build a typewriter for commercial use. The typewriter

Christopher Sholes

Source: Wikimedia Commons

eventually gained widespread popularity, and it's easy to see why: the average typist could produce about three times as many words per minute as someone writing by hand.

Mergenthaler saw the potential for adapting the typewriter to his invention. An operator would type the letters, which were directed into a lead mold to be printed, then returned to their original position to feed the next line. It became a continuous process. His invention fueled the growing newspaper business. The numbers vary according to different sources, but there were at least 8,000 of his machines in use in 1901, and 70,000 by 1954. Previously, it was possible to set 1,500 pieces of type an hour; with this new invention, 5,000 pieces of type could be produced in that time. Mergenthaler continued to make improvements on what he would eventually call the Linotype machine.

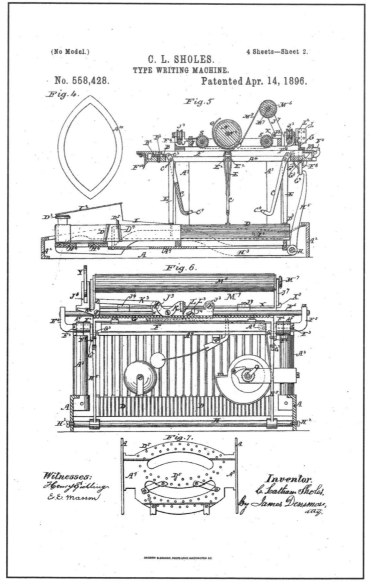

Patent No. US558428A for a typewriting machine by Christopher Latham Sholes

HOW DO YOU SPELL "QWERTY"?

Have you ever wondered why the letters on your keyboard aren't in alphabetical order? The first typewriters actually were that way and were laid out in two lines, but the more frequently used keys kept jamming. After years of trial and error rearranging the keys and with the help of James Densmore, an educator who studied letter pairs, Sholes spaced the keys according to the frequency and patterns most commonly used, such as "t-h." The arrangement of the letters also made typing with two hands faster, which explains why after all these years it's still the keyboard we use today, including on computers and smartphones. Look at the first six letters from the left on the top row of your keyboard. That's how the keyboard we still use got its name: QWERTY.

According to Autumn Stanley's book *Mothers and Daughters of Invention*, women hold at least thirteen patents for improvements on the typewriter, including a typewriter for the blind, an uppercase attachment, and a reverse-movement attachment so you can go back spaces. In 1936, Beulah Louise Henry received a patent for a machine called the "protograph," which was an attachment to the typewriter that could produce four copies without the use of carbon paper. She also made improvements to the typewriter that enabled smoother feeding and better alignment of the document.

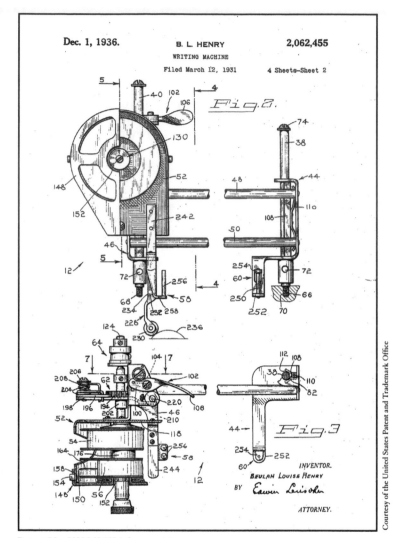

Patent No. US2062455A for a writing machine by Beulah Louise Henry

"Correction fluid" wasn't invented until 1956, when typist Bette Nesmith Graham experimented in her kitchen with paints and other substances to produce a fluid that could conceal errors on a typewritten page. According to some, Graham was inspired by watching a painter cover errors by painting over them using the same color as the background. Fellow typists quickly saw the benefit of covering over mistakes with Graham's "paint" and called it Paint Out. Later, Graham would perfect and market the mixture as Mistake Out and finally Liquid Paper, which she eventually sold to the Gillette Company for over forty million dollars.

Beulah Louise Henry at her typewriter

Source: Getty Images

After the field trip, I took my block of Linotype with my name and dipped it in fountain pen ink and tried printing with it. It printed poorly because the ink was too runny. My attempts to refill ballpoint pen cartridges with watery fountain pen ink also failed due to the wrong ink viscosity (thickness). My parents didn't always appreciate it, but as far as I was concerned, the whole house, from my mother's vanity to my father's basement workshop, was a laboratory for my experiments, including my investigation into the properties of liquids.

You can experiment with viscosity right in your own refrigerator by testing the consistencies of ketchup, syrup, milk, and juice. Here's how: Take four paper cups. Fill each one halfway with one of the liquids. Tip the glasses at different angles. You can easily observe how runny or thick the contents are. You can also mix the substances or add other substances to them, like flour, sugar, or mud. I should have tried mixing my ink with honey or syrup to make it thick, like Gutenberg's oil-based ink. It probably wouldn't have solved the problem completely, but it definitely would have been less runny.

The methods for making paper were still kind of basic when Gutenberg invented the printing press, but with the invention of movable type, there was a greater need for paper. The ability to mass produce books, newspapers, and pamphlets drove demand. Water-powered paper mills, which could pulp large amounts of wood in a short period of time, were the next step in paper production. The force of the water turns the blades of the wheel, which are connected to the machinery that turns the wood into pulp. These large mills were able to massively increase paper production by doing all the soaking, bleaching, pounding, and drying mechanically.

LIFE ISN'T ALWAYS FAIR

In 1799, the French inventor Louis-Nicolas Robert was awarded a patent for a machine that produced "continuous paper"; it was like a huge roll of toilet paper. When I was little, I used to love to pull the toilet paper roll and watch the sheets fly off in a stream. My mother would get very cross with me, but it's the best way I can describe what the continuous paper looked like coming off Robert's machine. He invented a rotating wire screen so that the paper pulp could be fed into a pair of rollers, producing a stream of continuous paper. Before Robert, paper was made by hand, one sheet at a time, and hung up like laundry to dry on the line.

Louis-Nicolas Robert worked for St. Leger Didot's paper company when he invented the continuous paper machine. He

Louis Nicolas Robert

and Didot fought over the rights to the patent. Robert had invented the machine, but Didot had supplied the money to develop it. Eventually, Robert sold his patent to Didot, who took it to England, where it was later perfected by the Fourdrinier brothers. They owned a stationery company and spent years improving on Robert's original idea. They put multiple rolls together (think of a head of hot curlers) through which the pulp would be drained. Excess water would be squeezed out, and then the pulp would finally be

Henry Fourdrinier

dried. This is the method we still largely use today to mass-produce paper. The new and improved Fourdrinier machine could not have been developed without Robert's original idea, but Robert died penniless, having sold his patent. The history of invention has its share of these stories, where the important

Source: Wikimedia Commons

Fourdrinier machine

contributions of early inventors get overshadowed by the people who figure out how to manufacture and market their work. It's not fair, but that's just the way it is.

Now that we know where paper comes from, let's get back to making snowflakes. The only other thing you'll need for making one is a pair of scissors. But don't take scissors for granted.

CUTTING EDGE

Scissors have been around for most of civilization. The first ones, which were invented by the Egyptians, looked more like shears: two blades attached at the base. The same basic design of two blades connected at the base has never changed, even though the design has been adapted to fit many needs, like farming, manufacturing, shearing cloth, cutting metal, and trimming candlewicks, just to name a few. There are even special scissors for cutting a baby's umbilical cord! Eventually, finger holes were added, and by the nineteenth century people were making beautifully decorated scissors with elaborate patterns decorating the blades and curlicues on the handles. The first company to manufacture scissors is still around today, producing scissors for every imaginable use: industrial, surgical, for textiles, cutting rubber, plastic, and even hair!

◁ ◁ ◁ **PAPER SNOWFLAKE** ▷ ▷ ▷

You'll need:

- Scissors
- 1 sheet of paper

To create:

1. Cut your paper into a circle.
2. Make three folds: First, fold your circle in half. It becomes a half-moon; fold that in half. Finally, fold the shape in half again.
3. Take your scissors and, all around the ends of your triangle, cut squares, circles, and more triangles. Use your

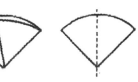

imagination for special effects.

4. Gently unfold your paper, and your snowflake will magically appear. Experiment with different types of paper such as vellum, patterned paper, or newsprint. Sheets of comic strip paper make very colorful and whimsical snowflakes!

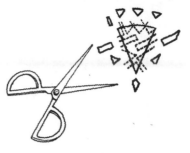

People often say that no two snowflakes are alike. Since no one can ever successfully study all the snowflakes in the world, that claim really can't be proven. To prove a scientific theory is true, you have to have "empirical evidence," which means you have to prove your idea by observing and experimenting. And you have to prove it over and over to make sure you always get the same result. Lawyers call this the "burden of proof." Scientists use a mathematical method called statistics to determine that the results are accurate and not due to random chance.

According to Kenneth G. Libbrecht, author and professor of physics at California Institute of Technology (and leading snowflakeologist), each snow crystal falls through the clouds on its own path to earth, which is why we think no two are alike. He further explains on his website SnowCrystals.com that a snow crystal (the more precise name for snowflake) is the result of water vapor turning to ice instead of becoming liquid (rain). All kinds of changes in temperature and humidity will affect the way the water molecules form to make the points of a snowflake, so even if they look the same when they land on your father's car, they will have microscopic differences. Still, they all have six "arms" because of the molecular structure of crystals, though one point or "arm" can be longer or thicker or "hairier" than the others. Professor Libbrecht, who was a consultant for the movie *Frozen*, has actually grown "identical twin" snowflakes in his lab, though even these, he says, are like identical human twins; they are never exactly identical.

◄ ◄ ◄ CRYSTAL SNOWFLAKE ▷ ▷ ▷

You'll need:

- Scissors
- 1 white pipe cleaner
- 2 cups boiling water
- Widemouthed canning jar
- ⅓ cup 20 Mule Team Borax detergent booster
- String or dental floss, 1 foot per snowflake
- Pencil
- 1 paper towel

To create:

1. Using your scissors, cut the pipe cleaner into three equal pieces and twist together in the middle to form a six-sided star.

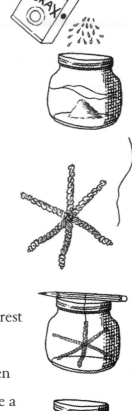

This will be the base of your snowflake.

2. Pour two cups of boiling water into the canning jar and add ⅓ cup of borax. Stir gently to dissolve.

3. Tie one end of the string or dental floss to the star shape and the other end to the center of the pencil.

4. Using the pencil like a fishing rod, lower the star into the jar of water, making certain the star is fully submerged but not touching the bottom of the jar. Then rest the pencil across the top of the jar.

5. Let your star sit overnight in the jar. When you check it in the morning, you will have a crystal snowflake! Remove gently from the jar and place on a sheet of paper towel to dry.

Note: If it does not work, try again. Other materials can be used. When I looked online, I found many instructions for making crystals from sugar.

Our teacher never used the word "symmetry," but that's what fascinated me about the snowflakes we created. Bilateral symmetry is when two opposite sides are exactly the same. Our faces are bilaterally symmetrical—so are eyeglasses, airplanes, and McDonald's golden arches. If you start looking around your classroom or your home, you'll start to notice things that are bilaterally symmetrical. Just looking around my apartment, I notice a baseball hat, a lamp shade, a round pillow, even the chair I'm sitting on. Once you start noticing, you probably won't be able to stop.

One Christmas, I got a present I really loved that reminded me of snowflakes, except the patterns were in Technicolor and kept shifting. It was a kaleidoscope. If you've never seen one, they are tube-shaped, like the inside of a roll of paper towels or a Pringles can. The inexpensive ones are made of cardboard, and I had one like that, but it seemed magical because it constantly produced new patterns. Inside kaleidoscopes, patterns are symmetrical. Mirrors are angled inside at one end of the tube, which creates the symmetrical effect when you peer inside and slowly turn the tube in your hands. The image inside will appear as a snowflake with six points. But then every little turn of the tube creates a new six-pointed crystal, which explains why I could look through mine for hours. It was like looking up at trees and watching the pattern of the leaves change when a cloud crossed the sun or when wind shifted the branches.

◁ ◁ ◁ **KALEIDOSCOPE** ▷ ▷ ▷

You'll need:

- Large, clean Pringles potato chips can with lid (10½ inches long)

- Darning needle
- Contact paper with sticky backing, or wrapping paper
- X-Acto knife
- Ruler
- 3-x-4½-inch thin acrylic mirror
- Masking tape
- Acetate (for example, clear vegetable containers)
- Stiff cardboard
- Beads, sequins, or miniature gems

To create:

1. Turn the Pringles can upside down and puncture a peephole in the metal end with the darning needle.

2. Decorate the outside of the Pringles can with contact paper or wrapping paper.

3. Use the X-Acto knife and the ruler to cut the acrylic mirror into three 3-x-1½-inch strips. Place the strips side by side (mirror side down) with a ¹⁄₁₆-inch space in between. Tape the mirror strips together with masking tape and bring the sides together (mirror side in) to create a tube with three flat sides—this is your prism.

4. Place the prism gently inside the Pringles

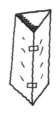

can; it should fit snugly so that the end of the prism is a half an inch from the can's opening.

5. To make the lens, use the base of the can to trace a piece of acetate the exact size of the can opening. Cut it out and lay the circular piece on top of the triangular prism.

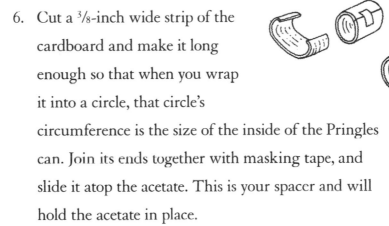

6. Cut a ³⁄₈-inch wide strip of the cardboard and make it long enough so that when you wrap it into a circle, that circle's circumference is the size of the inside of the Pringles can. Join its ends together with masking tape, and slide it atop the acetate. This is your spacer and will hold the acetate in place.

7. Fill the top of the container with your crystals, beads, and miniature gems. Do not fill completely in order to leave space for them to tumble and allow light in.

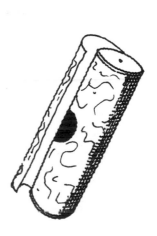

8. Cover with the plastic lid of the Pringles can so light can get in.

9. Look into the peephole, direct your kaleidoscope toward the light, turn slowly, and see what wonders appear before your eyes.

I was never very good at math, but I noticed that my paper snowflakes had repeating patterns that reminded me of the wheels of my bicycle, and sunflowers. Later, I discovered the term "radial symmetry," which mathematicians use all the time to describe these patterns. The patterns share two key features: they repeat themselves, and they fit inside a circle. If you look at the center of a sunflower, you will see that the seeds spiral in a systematic way. When people give examples of radial symmetry, they often mention snowflakes first because of their beauty. There are lots more examples of radial symmetry in nature, from tiny plantlike organisms called diatoms that live in the oceans to starfish, octopuses, orange slices, and the petals on a daisy. You can also find symmetry on your dinner plate if you're having broccoli, cauliflower, or artichokes. There's even a starfish called a chocolate chip starfish, which has radial symmetry: it fits inside a pentagram, which also fits inside a circle. If you use the image function on a search engine, you can find hundreds of photos of different types of symmetry.

Examples of radial symmetry

Source: Paul Shaffner via Wikimedia Commons

Source: Wikimedia Commons

DO THE MATH

....

A thirteenth-century Italian mathematician named Leonardo of Pisa, known as Fibonacci, discovered a mathematical sequence that explained the pattern of radial symmetry. According to historians, he was from a wealthy Italian family but was educated in North Africa. His father worked with merchants, and Fibonacci traveled all throughout the Middle

Fibonnaci

East. As a child, he studied accounting, learned the Indian symbols for numbers, and became fascinated by art. His ideas about this magical sequence of numbers came from the algebra and arithmetic he learned during his travels. His major contribution was bringing the Hindu-Arabic system of decimals and Arabic numerals (the ones we use today) back to Europe, which eventually took the place of Roman numerals and made modern mathematics possible. Fibonacci's sequence goes like this: You start with $1 + 1 = 2$. Add the last two numbers in the equation (1 + 2) to get the next number (3). You will see the pattern pretty quickly. Try it!

$$1 + 1 = 2$$

$$1 + 2 = 3$$

$$2 + 3 = 5$$

$$3 + 5 = 8$$

$$5 + 8 = 13$$

$$8 + 13 = 21$$

$$13 + 21 = 34$$

and so on.

The Fibonacci sequence is also called the "golden ratio" because these symmetrical patterns repeat both in nature and in man-made structures. Some scientists believe this mathematical theory was used in the building of the pyramids and Greek temples. Fibonacci's golden ratio also explains the spirals and curves in nautilus shells or pinecones or at the center of sunflowers. Mathematicians realized that these patterns form in nature so that plants and animals can grow in the most efficient way possible.

Source: Chris 73 via Wikimedia Commons

Inside of a nautilus shell

Fibonacci published his ideas in a book called *Liber Abaci* (*Book of Calculation*) in 1202, introducing the sequence to the Western world. This mathematical sequence would find many more applications in art, nature, and classical theories of beauty and proportion. Today, we apply the golden ratio to everything from the stock market to computer science to architecture and engineering.

To find cool visualizations of mathematics, use the "images" function on Google. Use keywords such as "geometry," "trigonometry," "fractals," "geometrical perspective," and "calculus." It's amazing to see how mathematics can be beautiful.

One last paper project we really loved as kids was water bombs, which I highly recommend if you want to extremely annoy a big sister or brother like I did when I was about seven years old. Believe it or not, regular printer paper will make a really good water bomb. The secret is coloring one side of the paper completely with crayons. The wax from the crayon will work as a seal and keep the water from saturating the paper. (Remember, wood fibers are broken down to make paper, so adding water will break down your paper unless it's wax coated.) You could also experiment with using candle wax or ChapStick.

▷ ▷ ▷

◁ ◁ ◁ **WATER BOMB** ▷ ▷ ▷

You'll need:

- 1 8½-x-11-inch sheet of paper
- Crayons
- Scissors
- Water

To create:

1. For an extra-strength water bomb, color one side of your piece of paper with crayon. The waxy coating will prolong the life of your water bomb. The colored side of the paper should be on the inside. You can also experiment with lining your paper with wax paper.

2. Using your scissors, cut the paper into a square. Fold the paper in half so it forms a rectangle, and then fold it in half again so it forms a square.

3. Fold one side of your square out into a triangle by following the arrow in the image to the right, and then flip over and do the same to the other side.

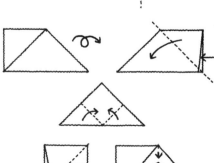

4. Hold the triangle so the right-angle point is at the top, and then, in both the front and the back, fold the bottom two corners of the triangle up so your paper is now diamond-shaped.

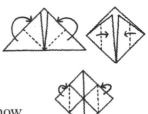

5. Next, take the outer two corners of the diamond in both the front and the back and fold them in to the center line.

6. Take the two loose flaps on the front and back of your folded paper and tuck them in to the pockets just below them.

7. You will see a little hole at the bottom end (the end opposite the flaps you just tucked in) of the water bomb. Blow gently to inflate like a balloon, and then fill with water. If the water from your faucet flows too fast, fill using a funnel or a straw.

"EVERYTHING IMAGINABLE"*

....

When I was a child, I had a box of Crayola crayons that had eight colors: red, orange, yellow, blue, green, black, brown, and violet. People have been mixing waxes and pigments through-out history and across cultures, but in 1902, a husband and wife duo, Edwin Binney and Alice Stead Binney, developed a nontoxic mixture mostly made of paraffin wax and natural dyes that were safe for children to use. Edwin was a partner of a chemical company with his cousin C. Harold Smith, and Alice was a schoolteacher. It was she who suggested they develop an inexpensive coloring tool and came up with the name "Crayola" by combining the French word for chalk, *craie*, with "ola" from the word "oleaginous," meaning oily. Alice's hunch turned out pretty well. Today, there are 120 colors, and 3 billion crayons are made each year.

Crayola company motto.

I waited for just the right moment with my water bomb, hiding behind the slide in the playground. I was a little nervous because the crayon coating would only work for so long. Then, just when my sister was in reach, I launched my water bomb, and it landed on her back, completely soaking her. My ambush was a success, except that my sister ran inside and told Mother that I'd thrown a wet box at her. I no longer remember my punishment, though I'll never forget the feeling of watching that water bomb fly through the air toward its target. Officially, I recommend throwing your water bombs against a tree or the side of your house. Unofficially, siblings are more fun.

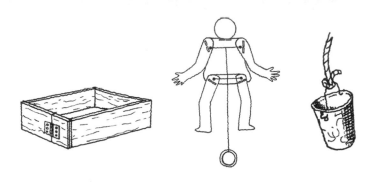

• CHAPTER TWO •

LEVERS AND PULLEYS

I used to ask my grandfather science questions all the time like *Why is the sky blue?* and *Why is grass green?* Most parents usually don't know or have forgotten the answers to questions like that, but my grandfather was an engineer and inventor, and he would explain that the Earth's atmosphere has an effect on the sun's color spectrum, which is why the sky is blue. As he explained this, I visualized a picture that my elementary school teacher had shown us of the solar system. We had learned that the Earth's atmosphere is very thin. If the Earth were an apple, the atmosphere would be its skin. While thinking about this, I visualized a childhood picnic I was at when I saw a smokestack making a swirl of dirty black smoke against a blue sky. I asked several adults if the smoke would make the air darker and dirty. I was told that it just disappears, but I did not believe it. I could visualize the atmosphere as being thin like the skin of an apple, and I knew the dirty smoke would get trapped beneath it.

Ever since I was young, I connected words with pictures, which is why I can easily translate abstract ideas into detailed drawings like the ones I made for engineering projects. The first books your parents read to you probably connected pictures to words. Learning the word for the image was the point: apple, ball, cat, and so forth. In school, we are also taught to learn with words first. But for me, words were always less important. If I can picture something, I can understand it. And then I can create it. There are many different kinds of learners and thinkers. Some people, like mathematicians, easily see patterns and sequences; lines of complex musical notations will make more sense to a person with a mathematical mind than to someone who primarily learns through words or pictures. According to biographer Walter Isaacson, Einstein "generally preferred to think in pictures." He recounts a conversation Einstein had with a

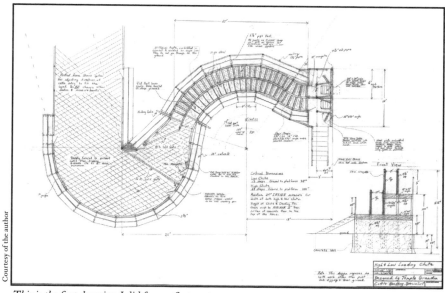

Courtesy of the author

This is the first drawing I did for my first customer.
It's a drawing of a cattle truck loading ramp.

psychologist, Max Wertheimer, who studied perception: "I very rarely think in words at all," Einstein said. "A thought comes, and I may try to express it in words *afterwards*."

My grandfather stimulated my early interest in science and invention. There may even be a genetic link that explains our shared interest. You can look up one of his patents, Patent No. US2383460A, for a magnetic field responsive device. His invention makes the autopilot on airplanes work. A really fun thing to do online is to look

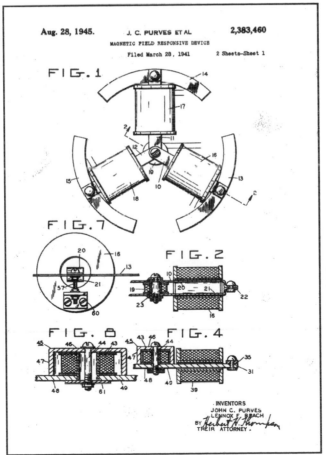

Patent No. US2383460A for a magnetic field responsive device by John C. Purves

up patents. You can easily find any invention; just type in "Google patent" and enter key words for whatever you're interested in. It's much easier to search Google than the government patent site, though you can use that, too.

Our Founding Fathers passed the first patent act in 1790, protecting "any useful art, manufacture, engine, machine, or device, or any improvement thereon not before known or used." The three men on the original patent review board were then Secretary of State Thomas Jefferson, our first attorney general, Edmund Randolph, and our first president, George Washington. The originator of an invention could file a patent that prevented other people from copying it for a period of twenty years. It's interesting to think that the freedom to invent was linked with our country's founding principles. If you've ever wondered how America has been at the forefront of so much innovation, part of the answer is the very freedom our country is founded on, which includes the freedom to invent, market those inventions, and protect the inventor's work. The Founding Fathers understood and valued the fact that a free, creative, and entrepreneurial spirit fuels progress.

FAMOUS FIRSTS

The first U.S. patent was granted in 1790 to Samuel Hopkins for a new apparatus and process for making potash, which consisted of wood ash and salt, and was used in making fertilizer. Women were not barred from applying for patents, but since most women couldn't legally own property independent of

Source: Wikimedia Commons

Samuel Hopkins

their husbands, by extension they didn't own the rights to their inventions. This would eventually change when New York State became the first to allow women to apply for patents and keep the profits from their inventions. These ownership rights were extended state by state under what is known as the Married Women's Property Act of 1848. In 1908, Mary Kies was the first woman to be granted a United States patent. She didn't invent hats, but she developed a process for weaving straw and silk to make them. First Lady Dolley Madison praised the hats, and her endorsement really helped the hats sell, sort of like when Michelle Obama wore clothes from J.Crew and spiked their popularity.

Until 1940, only twenty other patents were awarded to women. Adrienne Lafrance, in a 2016 article in *The Atlantic*, reported that women received a fraction of the patents that men received over the next two decades and they were mostly for domestic inventions, or things for the home, which makes sense since most women still didn't go to college or get jobs outside the home. For example, women invented new kinds of fireplaces and cookstoves, a hand-cranked ice cream maker, disposable diapers, dishwashers, and the foot-pedal trash can. In her early twenties, Beulah Henry received her first patent in 1912 for a vacuum ice cream freezer, which basically insulated the wall of an ice cream maker to keep the ice cream from melting. Also known as Lady Edison, she invented more than one hundred inventions including a hair curler, continuously attached envelopes, a snapping mechanism used on umbrellas, and can openers. She was known for saying, "I invent because I cannot help it." Though the number of women patent holders has increased, according to Lafrance, to about 20 percent, at the rate we're going now, it won't be even between men and women until 2092! Girls, we've got work to do!

The first patent awarded to an African American man was in 1821, for a process known as dry-scouring (think dry cleaning). Thomas Jennings was born a free man in New York City and as a result was able to obtain a patent. He was a tailor by trade and then started a dry-cleaning business. Slaves were not yet allowed to patent their own inventions; in fact, their masters could claim their inventions as their own. It wasn't until the passage of the Thirteenth Amendment abolishing slavery that all African Americans could patent their inventions. Jennings worked his whole life, both to free members of his family and as an activist, holding the position of assistant secretary to the first annual Convention of the People of Color.

Sources vary about who was the first African American woman to receive a patent. Most cite Sarah E. Goode, who, in 1885, after having been granted her freedom in the Civil War, invented the "hideaway bed," a fantastic space-saving device that looked like a rolltop desk. Goode was the daughter of a carpenter and the wife of an upholsterer and stairmaker. Eventually, she opened a furniture store. Goode's bed looked like a rolltop desk with storage space and became popular as more people were moving to cities and living in cramped quarters. Her invention would inspire the later Murphy bed, which folded up into a wall to create living space. The Greek

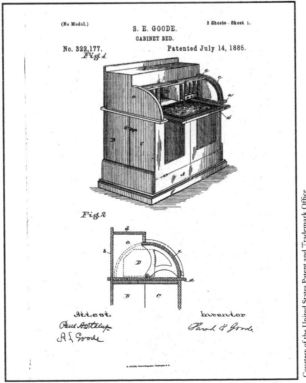

Courtesy of the United States Patent and Trademark Office

Patent No. US322177A for a cabinet bed by Sarah E. Goode (To see how it turns into a bed, you will need to look up the patent.)

philosopher Plato is sometimes credited with the saying that "necessity is the mother of all invention," which is a great way to think of how inventions come into being. Where there is a need, there is an inventor.

FOUNDING INVENTOR

Everyone knows Thomas Jefferson as the man who drafted the Declaration of Independence and served as our country's

Source: The White House Historical Association Digital Library via Wikimedia Commons

Thomas Jefferson

third president. But not everyone knows that he was a lifelong inventor as well. Among his more famous inventions is an improved "moldboard," which is the curved metal blade on a plow that turns the land over, especially for the kind of hilly terrain of his Monticello (Italian for "little mountain") estate. Henry Blair, the second black patent recipient, received a patent in 1834 for a seed planter that improved on the plow by combining tilling and seeding the land. His invention looks like a wheelbarrow with a compartment to hold the seeds and a rake that drags behind to cover them. He received a second patent that improved his invention yet again by attaching two blades to split the ground as the wagon was pulled through the soil so the seed would go directly in. A third inventor, George Washington Carver, was born into slavery in 1864 or 1865 (his exact birth date is not known) and was freed as a child. He made an even greater contribution to farming by recognizing the importance of rotating crops so that the land doesn't become depleted of nutrients. A student of botany and agriculture, Carver received a master's degree from Iowa Agricultural College and became the director of the Tuskegee Institute, where he developed hundreds of uses for peanuts and potatoes. Carver, however, only obtained three patents in his life, saying, "God gave them to me. How can I sell them to someone else?"

George Washington Carver

Source: Tuskegee University Archives/Museum via Wikimedia Commons

Jefferson made all sorts of labor-saving devices, such as a five-sided revolving bookstand so that he could look at multiple books at once. (I think

Source: Library of Congress, Manuscript Division

Thomas Jefferson's pasta machine and notes

he would have loved e-books.) He invented other devices that also involved rotation: a rotating clothing rack, a swivel chair, and a revolving-service door, which was a precursor to the lazy Susan. But he didn't stop there. Jefferson is credited with inventing one of the all-time great foods right up there with pizza and hot dogs: macaroni and cheese. You can see his notes on making pasta and his pasta machine.

The idea of patenting inventions is not new. One of the earliest patents was in Florence, Italy, in 1421. It was for a crane that could move pieces of marble through the mountains. In 1624, a law was passed in England that in order to file a patent, the invention had to be new and novel. Slight alterations of existing designs, such as changing the patterns on playing cards, could not be patented.

The good news is that there is no age limit to apply for a patent in the U.S. today. You can get a patent no matter how young (or old) you are. In 2008, Sam Houghton, at five years old, became the youngest patent holder on record. He saw his dad sweeping with two brooms, one to pick up the big stuff and another for the small. He thought he'd make his work easier by rubber banding the two brooms together. He was awarded a patent for his Sweeping Devise with Two Heads.

Rob Lammle compiled a list of the youngest inventors on the website Mental Floss. One fifteen-year-old skater needed something to keep his ears warm so he could stay out longer on the ice. Chester Greenwood devised a wire to go over his head and hold earmuffs in place. He got a patent for "ear mufflers" in 1877. Louis Braille was blinded at age three, and, by age fifteen, developed the system named after him that is still in use today for teaching the blind to read. Becky Schroeder is said to be the youngest woman to receive a patent. At ten, she created something she called a Glo-sheet, a sheet of paper that glowed in the dark. At twelve, she got a patent for "Electro-luminescent backing sheet for reading and writing in the dark."

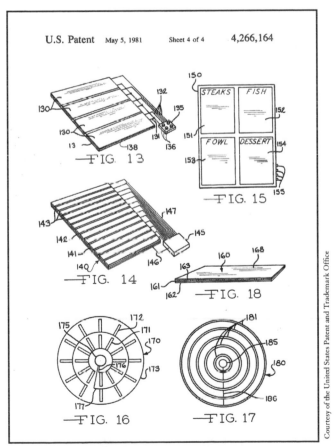

Patent No. US4266164A for an electroluminescent backing sheet for reading and writing in the dark by Becky Schroeder

IN THE BAG

....

As a girl, Margaret Knight, like me, preferred to play with tools and make toys rather than play with dolls. Known as a "woman Edison," she received over twenty-five patents for inventions as various as a machine for cutting shoes, a numbering device, a barbecue spit, and a window sash. In 1850, when she was twelve years old, she was visiting her brothers at a local cotton mill when she witnessed a terrible accident. A steel-tipped shuttle, which holds the yarn and is passed between the strings of a loom, went flying off the machine and injured a young boy. She devised a safety device that, according to Avil Beckford's website, The Invisible Mentor, turned off the machine when something malfunctioned. Her device was copied by cotton mills throughout the country. She didn't get a patent for her invention or profit from it, but more importantly, it prevents accidents and possibly saves lives.

Knight was thirty years old when she was awarded her first patent on May 18, 1879, for a machine that manufactured flat-bottomed paper bags, like the kind I used to take my lunch to school in, or that are still used today at supermarkets. Her invention was so ingenious and potentially profitable that another inventor, Charles F. Annan, copied it and applied for a patent first. No longer a twelve-year-old girl with no recourse, the forty-one-year-old Knight fought back, taking Annan to court. He claimed that, as a woman, she wouldn't be capable of the sophisticated knowledge required to build the machine to make the bags. Knight, armed with all her notes and notebooks, was able to prove her intimate knowledge of the machine at every stage. She won her case.

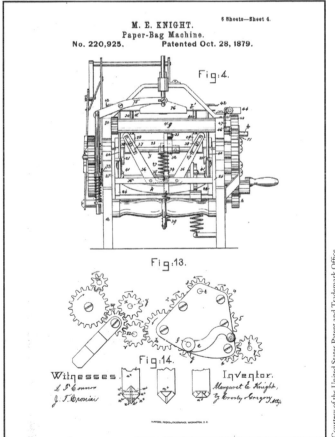

Patent No. US220925A for a paper bag machine by Margaret E. Knight

THE TUBE

· ·

We have Philo Farnsworth to thank for the television. By all accounts, his extremely mechanical mind started figuring out how to use electricity when he was a child. He was thirteen when he converted his mother's hand-cranked washing machine and sewing machine to electricity. In high school, he won a national science prize for a theft-proof lock for car ignitions.

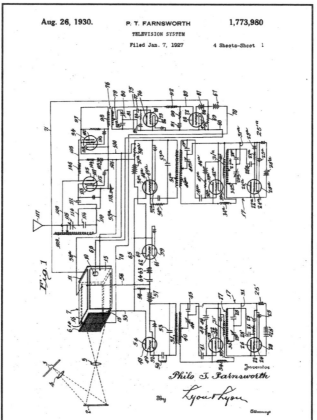

Patent No. US1773980A for a television system by Philo Farnsworth

Farnsworth was encouraged by a science teacher to develop his idea for transforming electricity into pictures, which he called

Source: San Francisco History Center, San Francisco Public Library

Philo T. Farnsworth

an "image dissector," essentially the first television system. You can still see the original sketch Farnsworth drew for his teacher that became part of his case for a patent, which he received in 1927 at the age of twenty-one. His claim states, "This invention relates to a television apparatus and process . . . for the instantaneous transmission of a scene or moving images of an object located at a distance in which the transmission is by electricity." Farnsworth imagined the television as a learning tool. He received over 130 patents over the course of his life, many showing improvements on his television system.

You can't patent things that have been around for zillions of years. You can't patent a table, chair, knife, fork, scissors, wheel, door, trousers, shirt, plate, or cup, to name a few. What you can patent are refinements to the original or "root" object. Patent laws have changed to include things like design changes, and this is where you will sometimes find thousands of small changes to an existing patent, many of which are valid and many of which, to my mind, seem frivolous. For instance, there are over 570,000 patent citations for toilet paper rolls, including a fancy toilet roll cover that looks like a muff. And some patents are just plain silly. For instance, a decorative fly-swatting device. Even the patent description is silly: "It is also believed that [flyswatters] would be more readily tolerated as 'sociable' household tools if only they were more attractive." I don't think this is quite what the Founding Fathers had in mind.

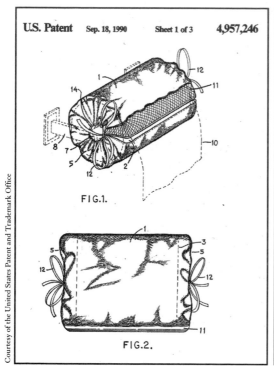

Patent No. US4957246A for a toilet roll cover by Karen D. Kantor

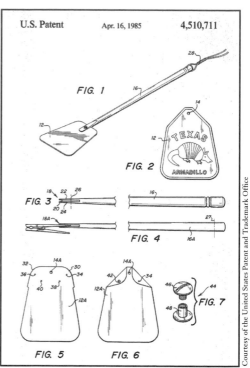

Patent No. US4510711A for a decorative fly-swatting device by David C. Bucek

One of civilization's oldest inventions is the lever. It has been around since prehistoric times and has been essential in the development of architecture and agriculture. Levers are so much a part of our lives that we barely realize when we are using one to open, cut, pry, lift, or build something. I first became interested in levers when I made a jumping-jack puppet. Because I'm a visual thinker, I've always loved anything that had rapid movement. If I had a choice between playing a board game and flying a kite, I would choose the kite. I just liked things that had parts and moved.

If you look around your house, you could probably come up with a list of things that use leverage to give you more strength than you naturally have. In my apartment, I can see a nutcracker, a bottle opener, a nail clipper, and scissors. A paint can is also a great example, though more specifically opening the lid. To pry it off, you slide the head of a screwdriver under the lip of the cover and push up and down the way you might have seen your parents pump the handle on a car jack if you've ever watched them change a flat tire. You will see that the lid comes up when you apply *force + distance*. Your arm pumping is the *force*. Holding the screwdriver at the farthest end from the can creates *distance*. This is how you create leverage: *Force + distance*. If you tried to open the lid with a coin, you wouldn't have enough leverage.

Your school playground or park has one of the best examples of leverage: a seesaw. I probably don't have to describe it, but it's basically a long board with a pivot in the middle, also called a "fulcrum." When you get on one end of the seesaw and your friend gets on the other, if you are the same weight, you will be balanced. If a bigger kid gets on, you know what happens: He or she stays on the ground and you go flying up. How would you bring the board back into balance? The bigger kid needs to move closer to the fulcrum. The lever does the work for you by exerting force on an object over a distance.

I once visited a class where I witnessed a student holding a hammer right near the head as he tried to hammer a large nail into wood. If you want the force and weight of a hammer to do its work, to push a nail through wood, you have to hold it at the end of the handle, or the "grip." The long handle provides greater hitting power. You may be more likely to miss the nail compared to using a hammer with a shorter handle, but for hammering large nails in, a hammer with a long handle is essential. If you need to tap in a small nail, you can gain control by holding the hammer closer to the head. The same idea is also used to pull nails *out* of boards. When you turn the hammerhead around and grasp the nail head in the claw, you hold the outer end of the handle to get the most leverage with the least effort. The length of the hammer handle is giving you more strength or force than you have on your own. It's the same principle with swinging a baseball bat. If you want to hit a home run, you hold the bat at the base or grip. This gives you the most power. If you want to bunt a ball into the infield, you hold the bat closer to the head, giving you the least leverage.

The first person who gets credit for describing leverage is Archimedes, who lived from 287 BC to 212 BC. He is considered to be the greatest scientist and mathematician of the Ancient World, but scientists believe that people have used the lever since the Stone

Archimedes

Shadoof

Age. Almost any feat of engineering and architecture relies on levers. Researchers believe that a form of lever called a *shadoof* was used in Egypt in the construction of the pyramids. Essentially, it is a pole with a bucket on one end and a counterweight on the other (think seesaw). Archimedes showed how you can lift a heavy weight with much less force by applying pressure to the long end of a lever. He is famous for saying, "Give me a place to stand and a lever long enough and I will lift the world!" Brilliant, but not too humble. Levers are a foundation of human ingenuity—how else could we have built buildings, dams, and roads, shipped goods, and done tons of other things?

You can't patent a lever, but patents for improvements on lifting jacks go way back. Canadian Frank L. Gormley Sr., who was born an orphan in Nova Scotia around 1881, moved to Harvey, Illinois, to work for the Buda Engine Company, manufacturers of railway supplies, including tracks, switches, signals, and jacks. When Gormley was approximately twenty-four, he invented a lifting jack that could lift 1,000 pounds. Without any formal training that we know of, Gormley went on to patent over twenty-five new improvements on the jack, things like a safety lock for lifting jacks, speed control for lifting jacks, toe-jacks, screw jacks, and so on. If you type his name into Google Patents, you can see all of them. He was clearly a brilliant man who worked at a plant that encouraged and rewarded innovation. I say this all the time because it's true: often the best education is hands-on.

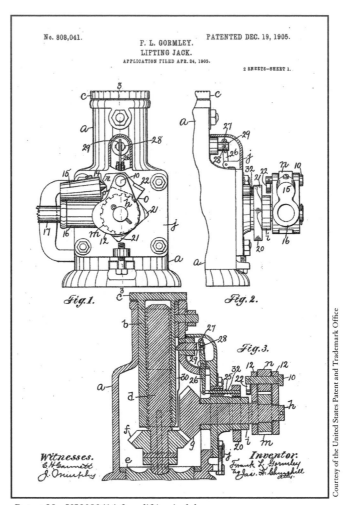

Patent No. US808041A for a lifting jack by Frank L. Gormley

CAN YOU GIVE ME A LIFT?

In 1884, an inventor named Richard Dudgeon was granted Patent No. US297975A for the hydraulic jack. Dudgeon was born in Scotland in 1819 and came to America as a young boy. He worked at the Allaire Iron Works company in New York City, which at the time was the largest ironworks company specializing in building steamships. Between his own natural aptitude and being exposed to the cutting-edge machinery of his day, Dudgeon eventually went on to start his own machine shop where he developed, in addition to the portable hydraulic jack, lots of other jacks and lifting equipment that helped shipbuilders and railroad engineers.

The hydraulic jack, as you have probably guessed, relies on water or liquid to supply the force. (Greek root *hydr* = water.) Two cylinders, one small and one large, are used to create leverage. When the small cylinder is pushed down, it forces the water underneath the large cylinder to go up and lift considerably more weight than a single person could lift. Remarkably, Dudgeon's company is still around today, and while their primary business is still levers, they are involved with incredibly sophisticated lifting machinery and work with organizations like NASA on things like their antenna-lifting projects. I think it's pretty cool for a company to be around for over two hundred years and put levers in space.

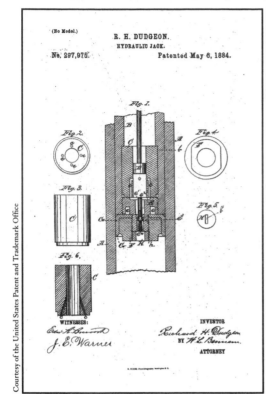

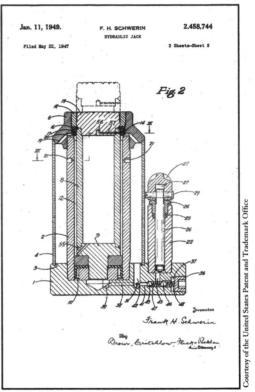

*Patent No. US297975A for a hydraulic jack
by Richard Dudgeon*

*Patent No. US2458744A for a simple
hydraulic jack by Frank H. Schwerin*

Jumping-jack toys use the simplest form of leverage and have
been around for a long time. The earliest ones that we know of were
found in Egypt and were made of ivory. In the mid-nineteenth-
century, jumping jacks were called "quocker wodgers," which was
also a nickname for corrupt politicians who could be manipulated
(the idea was that someone was pulling their strings or controlling
them like puppets). Jumping jacks became really popular among
the nobility in mid-eighteenth-century France, and were highly
decorated. They are too old to be patented, but I did find patents

that added some new features to them. In 1886, brothers John and Elmer Hersh patented a metal frame with a wood base and a wire that runs between the frame (think of a clothesline) that served as a pivot for the doll to jump around. In 1920, an inventor named Carl Olson created a metal case that two jumping jacks could swing through like trapeze artists. In his claim he states, "My invention relates to toys, and the object is to enlarge and improve upon jumping

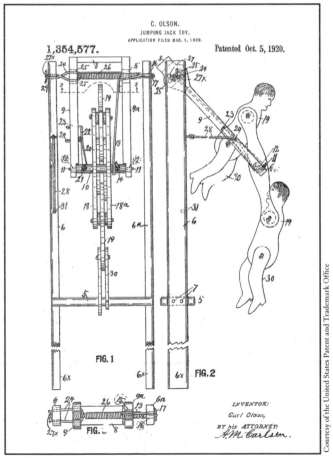

Patent No. US1354577A for a jumping-jack toy by Carl Olson

jacks and make them mechanically more perfect and capable of performing a greater number of feats and hence making them more interesting for children."

Jumping-jack puppets are easy to make out of cardboard, but you can also use balsa wood, Styrofoam board, or thin pinewood. You don't have to limit yourself to human figures; you can make jumping-jack animals like spiders, dogs, octopuses—pretty much any animal with legs that can bounce up. My drawing shows the basic principles without the decorations. Engineers call this a drawing that shows the "mechanical concepts." It shows where to attach the string in relation to the pivot points. Look at the dotted line: the arms go up two inches even though you've barely yanked the string a half

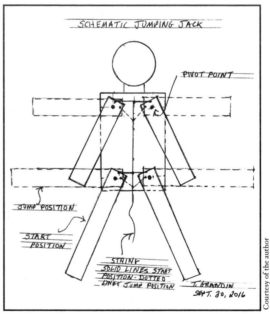

My schematic for a jumping-jack toy

inch. This is the simplest form of leverage—when the elements all move in the same direction, a small movement of the string results in the ends of the arms and legs moving a much greater distance.

▷ ▷ ▷

◁ ◁ ◁ **JUMPING JACK** ▷ ▷ ▷

You'll need:

- Pencil

- Heavy card stock, Styrofoam board, or balsa wood

- Scissors or sharp blade/crafting knife

- Marker

- Craft Pick or pointed scissors

- Paper fasteners

- String

- Curtain ring

- Felt, paper, and fabric, and ribbons or buttons

To create:

1. Use a pencil to draw each of the following body parts on the card stock, Styrofoam, or balsa wood: head, torso, arms, and legs.

2. Use the scissors (if you're using card stock or Styrofoam) or the sharp blade or crafting knife (if you're using balsa wood) to cut out each of the body parts. When put together, your jumping jack should be proportional. You can make it any size you wish.

3. Using the marker, place five Xs on the torso: one on each shoulder, one on each hip, and one where the neck would be (jumping jacks don't have necks). Also make Xs at the base of the head and the top of each limb.

4. With your Craft Pick or pointed scissors, poke a hole wide enough for a paper fastener to go through where you've drawn each of your Xs. Insert the paper fasteners through the holes, connecting the tops of the limbs to the torso and the head to the neck. Make certain the parts are not too tightly fastened together as you want them to be movable.

5. The next step is to attach the strings that will raise the arms and legs when the center string is pulled down. You'll need to attach one length of string to connect the arms to each other, and one length of string to do the same with the legs. Do not attach these strings to the pivot points. Experiment with different attachment points that are offset from the pivot points. It may not work the first time, and you

may need to do lots of experimenting. This will teach you how to be an inventor.

6. Take a length of string that matches the length of your jumping jack. Tie one end to the curtain ring and knot firmly. This will be your pull for the bottom of the jumping jack. Tie the other end of the string to the arm loop and the middle of the string to the loop of the legs and make sure there is no slack between the two loops you have connected.

7. Holding the jumping jack firmly, gently pull the curtain ring down, and your jumping jack will be a perfect example of leverage.

8. Have fun dressing your jumping jack in clothes made out of felt, paper, or fabric, and embellish with ribbons or buttons.

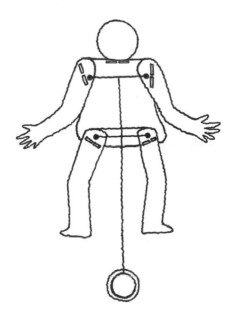

I found a 1927 patent that was actually granted for a candy jumping jack. You could probably figure out how to make your own using junk food like Twizzlers and Tootsie Rolls and sticks of gum for the arms and legs since they are soft enough to pull a needle and thread through but stiff enough to hold their shape. I imagine you could use a Peeps for the head and body, or maybe marshmallows. And then you can eat it. It sounds kind of fun, but I don't think it deserved a patent.

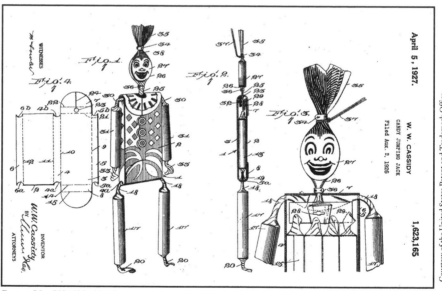

Patent No. US1623165A for a candy jumping jack by Willis Cassidy

Like levers, no one knows exactly who invented the pulley, but it's also one of humanity's most important discoveries and has been used throughout history to enable us to lift materials much heavier than ourselves. I first encountered this phenomenon in the horse barn at my boarding school. The hayloft had a trapdoor in the ceiling that was very heavy and never stayed open. The door was small, about five feet by two feet, with hinges on the narrow end. I devised a simple pulley to keep it open while I got the hay. I attached a hook on the opposite wall that I threaded a rope through. My own weight was enough to open it. A more complicated pulley system that uses multiple pulleys is known as "block and tackle" and is needed if you are lifting something heavier. The added pulleys provide a "mechanical advantage" by allowing you to lift greater amounts of weight. These are used on sailboats and cranes.

There are lots of uses for simple pulleys: wells, elevators, curtains, clotheslines, and flagpoles. Wishing wells use a simple pulley and are fun to make. All you need to make a wishing well is some clay or cardboard for the well and bucket, and some string or twine to hoist it up. You can even use dental floss! Nothing is off-limits when you're on the road to invention. You can also improvise a pulley with items you have around the house such as clothes hangers. I used pliers all the time to cut hangers and twist the wire into loops, which I used for some of my more complicated projects. I would work the pliers back and forth to create a deep enough dent in the wire so I could break it in half. The principle of leverage applies here, too. Squeezing the handles puts pressure on the head of the pliers and enables you to cut through things you couldn't break with your hands. You can also make a pulley out of a paper clip, pipe cleaners, buttons, or an old earring wire. Look in your family's junk drawer, and you'll probably find a lot of other things you could use.

◁ ◁ ◁ **SIMPLE WISHING WELL** ▷ ▷ ▷

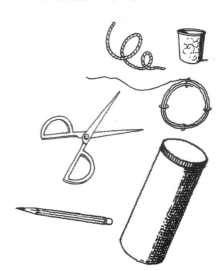

You'll need:

- Craft punch or sharp scissors
- Round oatmeal container
- Pencil
- Small Dixie cup
- 5-inch length of flexible wire
- Heavy-duty thread or string

To create:

1. Using your craft punch or scissor tips, punch two holes, opposite each other, toward the top of the oatmeal container. Thread the pencil through these holes.

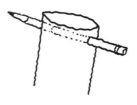

2. Again using your craft punch or scissor tips, make two holes in opposite sides of the Dixie cup, near the rim. Insert the 5-inch length of wire through the holes and twist the ends together to form your bucket handle.

3. Knot the string firmly around the center of the pencil. Attach the

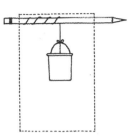

other end of the string to the wire on the bucket and knot firmly. When you turn the pencil, your bucket will lower and rise.

Another great pulley project is the curtain for a marionette theater. Set design is something I really loved in high school. When we did the Gilbert and Sullivan play *Trial by Jury*, I made a jury box and judge's stand from cardboard tacked to wood frames. Then I painted the cardboard to look like wood paneling in a courtroom by swirling brown paint using a stiff-bristle brush to create a wood-grain pattern.

To make the stage curtain, you need fabric that is heavier than a sheet but not as heavy as a blanket. Most theaters use velvet, and some have gold fringe. You can find these at a local sewing or craft store. Or perhaps your family has a box of rags or throwaway clothes. I'd plunder my mother's castoffs for all kinds of fabrics, especially her scarves when I started experimenting with making parachutes. Attics and basements usually have lots of stuff that's been discarded that you can salvage for projects. You have to have a scavenger mentality. You can also try thrift stores or tag sales. There's lots of treasure there. The more you can improvise, the better. I always loved the feeling of pulling the cord, watching the curtain part, and seeing the expectant faces of the people in the audience.

◀ ◀ ◀ PUPPET THEATER AND CURTAIN ▷ ▷ ▷

You'll need:

- Scissors or an X-Acto knife
- A large storage box or any oversize box
- Dowel, about 4 inches longer than the length of the front of the box
- Fabric for the curtain, a piece twice as wide as the length of your box front
- String
- Acrylic paints, markers, sequins, stickers, or pictures from magazines
- Christmas lights or flashlights

To create:

1. Using your scissors or X-Acto knife, cut out the front of the box as shown in the illustration.

2. The dowel will serve as your curtain rod. Punch holes half an inch apart across the top border of the fabric, approximately an inch from the edge.

3. Use your string to make a loop for each of the holes. The loops should be a little bigger than the

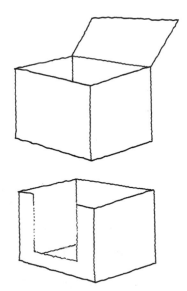

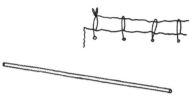

circumference of the dowel. Run
the dowel through the loops. Now
run another piece of the string
through the loops and tie it to
the last loop. When you pull this
string, it will pull the curtain back.

4. Use the tip of your scissors or an X-Acto knife to
   create a hole on each of the "walls" of the theater
   opening, one inch below the
   "ceiling"—large enough to fit the
   dowel snugly. Insert the two ends
   of the dowel into the two holes you
   have created.

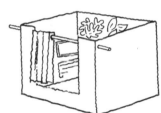

5. Decorate your theater with acrylic
   paints or markers. You might also
   try sequins, stickers, and pictures
   from magazines. Try to make a marquee with the
   part of the box you have cut out.

6. You can light your theater with Christmas lights or
   flashlights.

My first true invention as a teenager involved pulleys and leverage. It didn't come to me all at once. In fact, my first attempt was a
total failure, and I gave up on it for a few weeks. It was the 1960s,
and I was at my aunt Ann's farm in Arizona for the summer. As

I've said, this is where my interest in cattle formed. Every aspect of that farm fascinated me and informed all the choices I would later make in my career and life. But that summer, there was a recurring problem with the horses and cattle: they kept escaping from the farm.

There is a piece of farm equipment called a cattle guard, which is used to keep cows from crossing out of your property. It's basically a grid of bars that lays in the ground over a pit. The cattle guard enables cars and trucks to drive through the ranch entrance and not have to stop to open gates, but prevents horses and cattle from doing the same because they can see the deep pit under the bars and they are afraid to cross. This is called the "visual cliff effect." The grating does not hurt the animals' feet, but it is slick, which also makes the animals hesitant to walk on it. Over time, the pit fills in with dirt and debris, and as a result horses and cattle are no longer afraid to cross. On the farm, adding to the cows' innate desire to roam, there was a bull named Eli Whitney (named after the inventor of the cotton gin) in the next pasture, and our animals liked to visit his ranch.

So I went about building a gate out of two-by-fours, which is a standard-size piece of lumber that builders regularly use. The first step was bolting them together. In high school, we did a lot of carpentry, and by then I knew how to use saws and hammers, and I was able to design and construct the gate. I had already shingled a barn roof and framed a house. The gate posts were made of cross beams salvaged from old electrical poles. I did everything myself except for digging the holes and filling them with concrete to anchor the posts in the ground.

It was a manual gate, and I was quite proud of it. It did the job of keeping the cows and horses in our pasture. However, it also fell to me to jump in and out of our pickup truck to open and close the gate every time we drove through. So I decided to find a way to make it an automatic gate. At the time, the farm didn't have electrical wiring that reached all the way to the driveway, and people weren't using solar-powered equipment yet. Maybe because we didn't have any fancy gadgets or Home Depots to poke around in back then, I kept it simple. Since then, I've learned many

Me building a gate at my aunt's farm

Courtesy of the author

times on many jobs that the first rule of design is to keep it simple. Sometimes when my students are developing experiments to observe and test animal behavior they start to complicate it with unnecessary steps and come to me for advice, and I always have them simplify their experiments. Albert Einstein famously once said, "Everything should be made as simple as possible, but no simpler." I completely agree.

KEEP IT SIMPLE

....

Part of any scientific method, which is testing a hypothesis to see if it's true and accurate, is figuring out the most efficient way to collect data. When studying animals, we use "continuous observation" to record all kinds of behavior: sleeping, eating, fighting, mating, grooming, and even peeing and pooping. When I was getting my Master's degree, I was assigned to observe an animal for half a day. I could have stayed on campus and watched squirrels running around, but I went to the zoo and decided to observe the antelope. Unlike the smaller animals in cages, the antelopes were in a big enclosure, and I thought they might exhibit more natural behavior as a result. I found a spot and stayed there for four hours or so. The one behavior I still vividly remember was when they came up to the fence and stuck their horns through, sparring with each other. They only did it a few times, so if I had only watched for an hour I would have missed this essential display of dominance hierarchies, which shows which animal has the highest ranking. My patience was rewarded. Results take time.

These days we often use video to document animals 24/7 so we can see what they are doing night and day. At first my students were excited about the data we would collect until they realized they would have to spend weeks watching the videos just to document how often the cattle pooped. I explained a simple method where you fast-forward the video, which saves a lot of time collecting the data. For instance, to determine how often they poop, you count how often their tails fly up in the air, which is what cows do to keep their tails clean when they go to the bathroom. A tail flying up is easy to see on the sped-up videos. Fast-forwarding is a simple solution to allow you to watch hours of video more quickly. The best solutions often are simple.

The first step was to hang the gate on a slightly crooked hinge so that after it was opened, it would automatically swing back to close. I had observed this on doors in older houses when they sagged and settled. I fastened the hinges to the gatepost on a slight angle, and it worked really well: when I let go of the open gate, it swung closed.

The next step was to develop a cable and pulley system so the driver could jerk the gate and cause it to swing wide open. This would also provide enough time for a car to drive through before the gate closed. I ran the cable from the lever to the gate farthest away from the hinges. No matter how hard I pulled on the cable, the gate would not open far enough. At this point I did no further experimentation. I was really frustrated. My magic gate was a failure.

Inspiration comes when you least expect it. A couple of weeks later, I found myself watching the moving flaps on the heating vents in my aunt's house. When I moved the lever on the vent a short distance, the end of the metal flap that closes off the vent moved a much longer distance. I immediately made the connection between the metal flap and my gate. This is what I call my "light bulb moment." I've heard lots of scientists talk about their light bulb or aha! moment. Sometimes it comes after years of research, sometimes it takes another person to look at a situation to see what has been right in front of you, sometimes it just mysteriously clicks. Finding the eureka! moments requires good observation. The vent flap was my inspiration for making the magic gate work.

I reasoned that if I attached the cable closer to the hinges, the cable could be pulled a shorter distance and the door would open at a longer distance. You can see that putting

Courtesy of the United States Patent and Trademark Office

I got the idea for attaching the cable that opened my gate closer to the hinges from an air register on my aunt's ranch. This patent (No. US160514A) shows a similar hot-air register.

the pivot closer to the hinge supplied the leverage so that the cable could be pulled a shorter distance to swing the gate open.

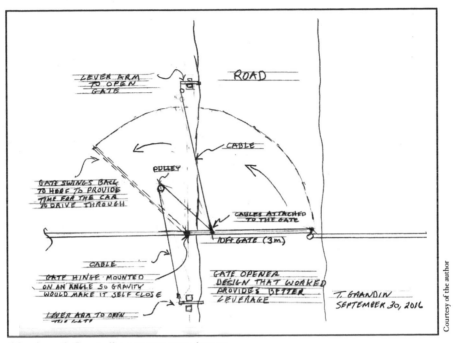

LEVER ARM
TO OPEN
GATE

ROAD

CABLE

PULLEY

GATE SWINGS BACK
TO HERE TO PROVIDE
TIME FOR THE CAR
TO DRIVE THROUGH

CABLES ATTACHED
TO THE GATE

10 FT GATE (3m)

CABLE

GATE HINGE MOUNTED
ON AN ANGLE SO GRAVITY
WOULD MAKE IT SELF CLOSE

LEVER ARM TO OPEN
THIS GATE

GATE OPENER
DESIGN THAT WORKED
PROVIDES BETTER
LEVERAGE

T. GRANDIN
SEPTEMBER 30, 2016

My schematic for a pulley system to open the gate

◁ ◁ ◁ SMALL CORRAL WITH ▷ ▷ ▷
SELF-CLOSING GATE

You'll need:

- Handsaw
- 1 1-inch-thick piece of 32-x-4-inch wood
- 1 ¼-inch-thick sheet of 8-x-8-inch plywood
- Wood glue

- ½-inch x ⅝-inch brass butt hinge
- 6 each #1 Phillips screws
- Phillips screwdriver

To create:

1. With the handsaw, cut the 32-x-4-inch wood into four 8-inch pieces. Take one of the 8-inch pieces and cut it to form one 5-inch piece and one 3-inch piece.

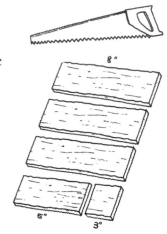

2. Place your 8-x-8-inch plywood on a flat surface. Glue three of the 8-inch pieces of wood you just cut with the saw upright onto three sides of the plywood (so that they're against the sides and not on top at the edges). One side will remain open.

3. Join the 5-inch piece of wood and the 3-inch piece together at the spot where they were cut apart by attaching the brass butt hinge between them using the screws and screwdriver. This will form the gate to your fenced area. You can experiment with how to attach this to make the gate self-closing.

4. Glue the 5-inch part of hinged section onto the open front of the

plywood, once again against the side of the plywood. Be sure to position this section so that the 3-inch piece can swing outward. If you want the gate to close automatically, affix the hinge on a slight angle, like I did with the gate at my aunt's ranch.

ACCIDENTS WAITING TO HAPPEN

Many discoveries in science are accidental. One that has saved billions of lives was discovered by Scottish scientist Alexander Fleming when he left a petri dish uncovered in his lab. Throughout World War I and the beginning of World War II, Fleming wanted to help wounded soldiers whose infections were often more dangerous and sometimes fatal than the wounds themselves. He had been experimenting with the healing properties of bodily secretions like tears, mucus, and phlegm.

Then, in 1928, returning from a vacation, Fleming noticed that one of his petri dishes had been left open, and there was a mold growing inside it. Fortunately, he didn't throw it in the garbage but instead put it under the microscope. The bacteria in the dish had been killed by the fungus. What he first called "mold juice" became what we now know as penicillin. It was developed in time to save many lives in World War II, and Fleming was awarded the Nobel Prize. His discovery is among the greatest of modern medicine. The next time you see moldy bread or mold growing on something in nature, don't be grossed

Source: Wikimedia Commons

Alexander Fleming

out. Take a sample and stick it under a microscope. "Everywhere I go people want to thank me for saving their lives," said Fleming. "I really don't know why they do that. Nature created penicillin. I only found it."

Inventor Stephanie Kwolek sounds a little like me. According to the Chemical Heritage Foundation, she loved exploring the woods as a child and making scrapbooks of the specimens she found there. She also loved fabric and sewing. Combining her hands-on experience with her scientific mind, she became one of the first women to work at DuPont, the chemical company most well known for developing the first synthetic (human-made) fibers, such as nylon. Kwolek started at DuPont in 1946 and was assigned to a team of chemists who were trying to develop a stronger, more lightweight material than the steel used in tires. They were testing all kinds of ways to convert the substance polymer into a liquid when Kwolek zeroed in on a milky solution headed for the trash. According to her obituary in the *New York Times*, her peers did not want to test the solution, but Kwolek persisted. Her hunch proved right, and as a result we

now benefit from Kevlar, the
synthetic fiber she discovered,
which is five times as strong as
steel and fire resistant, too. It has
saved thousands of lives as body
armor for police and the military,
and is used in everything from
suspension bridges to heavy-duty

Stephanie Kwolek

Photo courtesy of DuPont

rope, tires, safety helmets, fiber-optic cables, fire-resistant mat-
tresses, and much more. Like many before her, Kwolek didn't
profit from her discovery. She had signed over the patent royalties
to DuPont, who have greatly profited as a result of her brilliant
observation.

George de Mestral, a Swiss engineer, was hiking in the
Alps in 1941 with his dog. When he got home, he picked off
the burdock burrs sticking to his clothes and the dog. He put
the burrs under a microscope and saw that each thread of the
plant had a tiny hook at the end. That's where he got the idea
for what we now know as Velcro. It took him eight years (and
I'm guessing a lot of trial and error) before he introduced what
he called the "zipperless zipper." The name Velcro comes from
"velvet" and *"crochet,"* which means "hook" in French. The
original patent was filed in 1961 and called the invention a
Separable Fastening Devise. Mestral's obituary in the *New York
Times* points out that Velcro is "used for everything from keeping

astronauts from floating off the floor of their spacecrafts to keeping artificial hearts in place." If you go to Google Patents, you will find thousands of new uses for Velcro, including golf gloves, drink holders, and an anti-bed-wetting device. So the next time you're out hiking, pay attention!

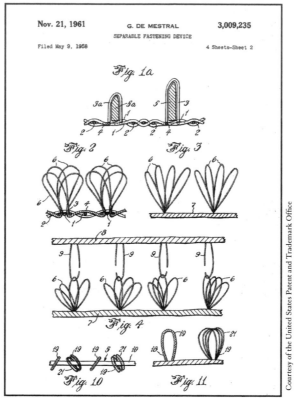

Patent No. US3009235A for a separable fastening device by George de Mestral

Sometimes you need different kinds of minds to bring different perspectives to a problem. You don't want to have one kind of thinker working on a project. You may need an engineer and a chemist and a psychologist to get to the bottom of something. I am often invited to consult at cattle-handling plants, zoos, feedlots, and all kinds of places where animals, for some reason, aren't functioning well. Because of my particular abilities with animals, my scientific background in animal sciences, and my years of experience, I can often figure out the problem. If it has to do with the facility, I'll need an engineer and an experienced person in the machine shop to execute the solution.

Similarly, when building an animal handling facility, we need the visual thinker (that's me) to lay out the whole building and invent the equipment. Then we need the millwrights and welders in the machine shop to build the equipment. We need engineers to devise the boilers, steam pipes, electrical systems, wastewater management, and refrigeration. I can't say it enough: we need all kinds of minds.

One last homemade toy I have to mention is an apple on a stick. It's probably the first (and nastiest) toy I used that really took advantage of leverage. Small crab apples grew in our backyard. All you do is put an apple on one end of a twelve-inch stick and throw it as hard as you can. Sometimes my siblings and I threw them at the next-door neighbor's house. You have probably guessed that it was the principle of leverage at work. By gripping the farthest end of the stick, your apple will go twice as far than if you threw the apple with your hand alone. I'm trying to make this sound scientific, but let's face it, we were just having fun.

• CHAPTER THREE •

THINGS MADE OF WOOD

When I was in the fifth grade, I was the second girl in my school who was allowed to take wood shop. Until then, wood shop was strictly for boys, and girls had to take cooking and sewing.

The very first thing I made out of wood was a violin plant stool. What, you might be asking yourself, is a violin plant stool? It's a good question. I have no idea how our shop teacher came up with the project, but it's a lot like it sounds: a stool meant to hold a potted plant, made out of a piece of wood cut in the shape of a violin. We could just as easily have been assigned a drum plant stool or a cat plant stool. Though in retrospect, he might have chosen it because it was a little complicated to saw the curvy S shape, and the whole point of the project was to learn how to use a coping saw. The coping saw has been around since the middle of the sixteenth century, and while there are lots of patents with improvements (different handles, motorized, and so on), the saw itself has pretty much remained unchanged.

JAGGED EDGE

....

A coping saw is made of a U-shaped frame. The two ends of the blade are attached to the tips of the U and are generally held in place with tiny screws. The blade, like all saw blades, has jagged teeth and faces outward. The value of this design is that you can cut intricate shapes into wood. The saw was really popular in the eighteenth century when elaborate designs, known as marquetry, were inlaid in furniture. Some of the designs remind me of the snowflakes we made in the first chapter. They are all about symmetry. We did not cut out the f holes in the violin, named for the f-shaped opening on either side of the strings, used to help amplify the sound. Cutting the holes would have required taking the coping saw apart and threading the blade through a hole drilled in the wood, but if you've ever wondered how holes are cut in wood, that's basically how it's done.

Coping saw

Source: Securiger via Wikimedia Commons

We made our violin plant stands out of soft pinewood, sanded the edges, and varnished the surface. The stool's legs were made from two triangles with the tops cut off. They were attached to the tabletop with two tiny finishing nails, so tiny that we only had to gently tap them in to secure the legs. You can experiment with different softwoods such as thin plywood and with all kinds of other shapes. With the glue we have now, such as Super Glue and Krazy Glue, you could easily glue the legs on. When I was growing up, we only had Elmer's glue, and it wasn't strong enough to attach the legs, especially if a potted plant had to be balanced on the stool.

◁ ◁ ◁ VIOLIN PLANT STAND ▷ ▷ ▷

You'll need:

- 1 sheet of 8½-x-11-inch paper
- Pencil
- Scissors
- 1 ½-inch-thick, 12-inch-x-9-inch piece of softwood, such as plywood or pine (if plywood is used, it can be ¼-inch thick)
- Coping saw
- Sandpaper (180 grit)
- Lightly dampened cloth
- 1 ³/₄-inch-diameter, 12-inch-long wooden dowel, a broom handle, or any cut pieces of wood about that size

- Wood glue
- Newspaper
- Clear-gloss varnish (acrylic or water-based) or a spray varnish
- Paintbrush (not necessary if using spray varnish)

To create:

1. Draw a violin shape onto your paper. The violin should be eleven inches long. It may be easier to draw half a violin on a folded sheet of paper. When it is cut out, it will be perfectly bilaterally symmetrical.

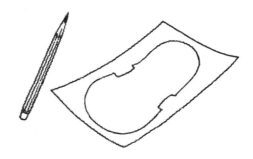

2. Cut out the shape and place it on top of your piece of wood. Trace around the edges of the paper onto the wood so you will see the violin shape outlined on the wood. Set the paper aside.

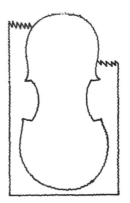

3. Using the coping saw, carefully cut out the violin shape from the wood.

4. Sand the edges of your wooden

violin shape with the sandpaper until the edges are rounded and smooth. Make certain that you sand in the direction of the wood grain. Clean the sawdust off the wood thoroughly with a lightly dampened cloth and let dry for half an hour.

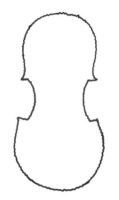

5. Cut the 12-inch dowel into four equal pieces, each 3 inches long. These are your stand's legs.

6. Mark the bottom of your stand with four Xs to indicate where the legs will be placed—each should be approximately an inch from the edge of the stand. Placing the legs near both ends will help to stabilize your table.

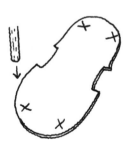

7. Attach the legs with wood glue. Allow to dry overnight.

8. Spread newspaper on the floor in a well-ventilated area. Place your stand on the newspapers. Apply the varnish with your paintbrush or from a spray can, applying in the direction of the grain. Allow to dry for 24 hours.

A SHORT HISTORY OF GLUE

You've probably used Elmer's glue. It comes in a white bottle with an orange cap and a cute bull as the mascot. Elmer the Bull was the Borden Company's logo. Someone in the marketing department dreamed him up as a companion for Elsie the Cow, the mascot of their dairy products. Like Minnie for Mickey Mouse, or Daisy for Donald Duck.

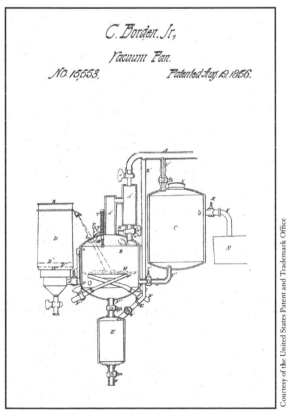

Patent No. US15553A for an improvement in concentration of milk by Gail Borden

The Borden Company was originally a milk delivery company. I can still remember the milkman delivering the

Source: Wikimedia Commons

Gail Borden

milk in glass bottles. Gail Borden invented a new process in 1856 to make condensed milk, which doesn't need refrigeration and won't spoil. Eventually, Borden became the biggest dairy company in America.

In 1939, Borden bought a company known for the Rotolactor, a machine that made it possible to milk a large number of cows at once. Invented by farmer and inventor Henry Jeffers, the machine, also known as the "rotary milking parlor," was hygienic *and* efficient. How it works is the cow steps into a stall on what looks like a merry-go-round, is washed and hooked up to automated milking tubes, and then steps off when it's done. Fifty cows get milked in the twelve and a half minutes it takes for the Rotolactor to make one revolution. Best of all, the cows remain calm throughout the process.

Borden first made glue in 1932 from a by-product of milk called casein. Early glue was sold in a glass bottle with a wooden stick like a Popsicle stick attached to the inside cover, kind of like the jars of paste you might have used (and possibly tasted) in kindergarten. Later, researchers found a formula

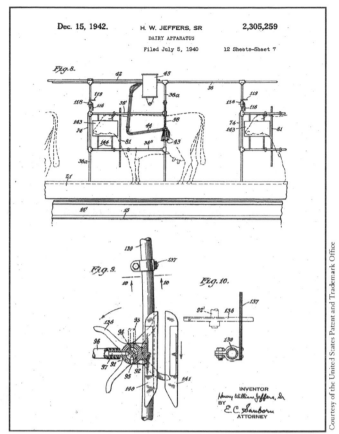

Patent No. US2305259A for a dairy apparatus by Henry Jeffers
(To see how the rotary system works, look up the patent.)

that included synthetic resins and developed the glue we still use today, along with the easy-to-squeeze plastic bottle and the orange cap that dispenses and then closes with a twist. You could spend days reading all the patents for squeeze-bottle caps. Just go to your refrigerator and compare the caps on your ketchup, mustard, and mayonnaise and observe the different designs. They're probably all patented.

The invention of Super Glue is another one of those great

stories of discovery-by-accident. The substance that makes Super Glue so crazy adhesive is cyanoacrylate. It's a form of plastic that hardens when it is exposed to air. In World War II, it was being developed as an alternative to stitches; scientists were trying to come up with something that could be applied more quickly on the battlefield to close wounds. But it was too difficult to use because the glue stuck to everything. Then, in 1951, two researchers at the Eastman Kodak Company, Harry Coover and Fred Joyner, also came across cyanoacrylate while testing hundreds of substances looking for a temperature-resistant coating for jet cockpits. They realized that the supersticky qualities of cyanoacrylate could be developed and marketed as the stuff we use today for gluing pretty much everything: glass, metal, leather, wood, and more. Super

Harry Coover

Source: The White House via Wikimedia Commons

Glue found widespread use as the glue of all glues. "Really it involved one day of serendipity and about ten years of hard work," said Coover in a television interview.

When I was growing up, there was a TV show called *I've Got a Secret*, where contestants had to guess a guest's career or what they were famous for. I liked it because sometimes the guest would be a scientist or inventor who brought along their invention. Harry Coover went on the show and, together with the host, was raised up into the air on a cable attached to two metal pieces held together by one drop of glue. It turned out to be one of the greatest publicity stunts of all time: the glue made history.

It was the mid-sixties and I was a student at the Hampshire Country School in Rindge, New Hampshire, when, for fun, I came up with the idea of making a homemade snowboard. There was a lot of construction happening on campus back then, and we often "borrowed" some of the materials that were lying around the construction site. I'm not sure how we never got caught, but one snowy winter we took an eighteen-inch-by-six-foot piece of smooth plywood paneling and nailed one end of it to the floor of our dormitory. Then we lifted the front of the board and shoved another piece of board under it, constantly wetting the wood to soften it and encourage it to warp. (You probably shouldn't try this at home—maybe because we were at boarding school we were more mischievous. My mother would have seriously punished me if I had nailed anything to the floor.)

It took about three days for the tip to warp enough to satisfy us, or maybe we just couldn't wait to get out there and try it. If you've ever used a snowboard or skateboard, you know that the front and back are both warped upward. The finished smooth side of the paneling went against the snow and we stood on the rough side for traction. The big difference between our board and the snowboards we have today are the boot bindings. We didn't have boot bindings! We flew down on those things like they were surfboards. Safe it definitely was not!

The first patent for a snowboard was awarded to Vern Wicklund and two brothers Harvey and Gunnar Burgeson in 1939. It is Patent No. US2181391A, and was filed under "sled." The patent states that the boards were an improvement on sleds and were used as a substitute for skis for jumping on snow or going over snowy ground.

There were probably lots of kids like us at Hampshire Country School who would fly down a snowy hill on just about anything, so it's hard to say exactly who invented the first snowboard. According to most sources, M. J. Burchett got credit in 1929 for making the first snowboard when he attached some clothesline and horse reins to a piece of plywood. Then in 1965, a man called Sherman Poppen, a chemical gases engineer, tied two skis together side by side and tied a piece of rope at the tip for his daughter to use. He manufactured this, calling his invention a Snurfer (snow + surf). It caught on for a while until 1969, when a college student named Dimitrije Milovich, who sounds a lot like me, became famous for sliding down hills while standing up on cafeteria trays. He dropped out of college and with Wayne Stoveken (who made up the phrase "snow surfing"), formed a company called Winterstick and created a board made of fiberglass with a fin-like piece of wood attached to the bottom of the board and two more on a diagonal at the back of the board. The fins made the board easier to control, and the board was patented in 1974.

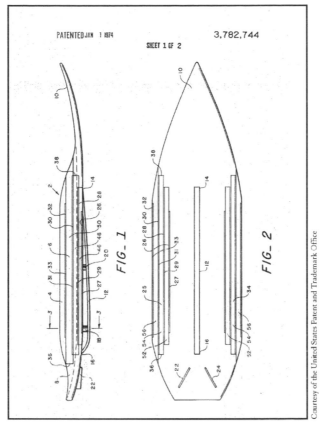

Patent No. US3782744A for a snow surfboard with stepped stabilizing sides by Dimitrije Milovich and Wayne Stoveken

Much as people loved surfing and skateboarding, the new sport that combined the two hadn't caught on yet. Then, in 1977, two men came on the scene with their innovations: Tom Sims and Jake Burton. Tom Sims made his first board in junior high school shop class with carpet on the top side and aluminum foil on the bottom. He became famous for introducing freestyle tricks and half-pipe competitions. He also built a company that made snowboards and gets credit for innovations like metal edges on the boards (just as he used tinfoil on his first board). If you've ever snowboarded, you've probably seen equipment with the name Burton on it. Jake Burton gets a lot of credit for his binding, though both men are listed on

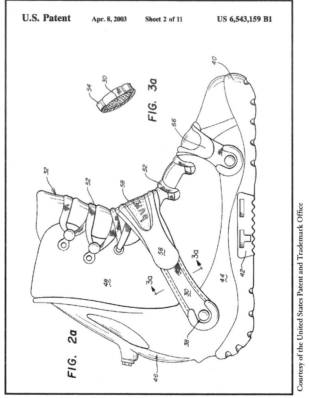

Patent No. US6543159B1 for a snowboard boot and binding strap by Jake Burton

quite a few patents for their contribution to the bindings. Today, almost as many people snowboard as ski, and that number goes up for people under age thirty-five. We were definitely on to something at Hampshire Country School.

Another project we made at boarding school from "borrowed" wood was giant stilts. We found some eight-foot-long two-by-fours and nailed footrests to them. You don't have to put the footrests up too high to get the fun feeling of towering over everyone. It is essential that the footrests are attached very securely to the two-by-four. I suggest you first start walking on your stilts in the grass to get the hang of it. If you're into sewing, you can sew pants or a costume to cover the entire length of the sticks. Or you can glue or use a staple gun to attach the clothes to the stilts.

I was a bit of a tomboy, but I made an exception for sewing. My mother had bought me a hand-cranked Singer Sewhandy in the fourth grade, and it fascinated me the way all machines with moving parts did. Plus, it was easy enough for a child to use; it's too bad it is no longer made. These days, most sewing machines are powered by electricity, which makes them dangerous for really small hands.

I'd use my Sewhandy to help our teacher make costumes for the school play. I volunteered all my free time, and I loved seeing the costumes worn by the student actors and actresses. When I discovered that the Sewhandy could sew crepe paper, I designed carrot costumes using wide green crepe paper sheets, which I pleated on one edge to make hats. To make them stand up, I bent the pleated section ninety degrees and used a string attached with Scotch tape to tie the hat onto my classmates' heads. Then I adapted the design and sewed the pleats into a waistband to make a skirt. I was always testing the limits, but I was very careful not to attempt anything that could damage my Sewhandy.

SEW WHAT

....

Elias Howe was the first inventor in my book of inventors who really impressed me, because I could connect his invention with something I directly used.

Elias Howe

He received the first United States patent for the sewing machine in 1846, though earlier versions already existed. According to the Museum of American Heritage and other sources, a British man called Thomas Saint first patented a sewing machine in 1790. It had the overhanging arm still used today, a straight needle, a continuous supply of thread, and a rotating hand crank. New Yorker Walter Hunt is credited with inventing the lockstitch, which improved on the chain stitch, which too easily unraveled. But it was Howe who put it all together: a lockstitch

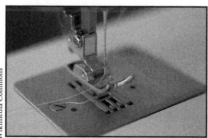

A sewing machine with thread running through the eye of the needle. The location of the eye near the needle's point makes a sewing machine work.

that is formed above and beneath the cloth, an automatic feed for the fabric, and his own ingenious design of placing the needle with the eye at the point of insertion into the fabric. It seems like a tiny thing—the eye of a needle—but it contributed to the industrial revolution by producing clothes faster and more cheaply.

Howe had a hard time finding investors for his sewing machine and went abroad to seek funding. What happened next is similar to the case of Louis-Nicolas Robert's continuous paper machine. Unfortunately, it's not uncommon for an original inventor's contribution to be overshadowed by the people who have the money and ability to manufacture and market the product. When Howe returned to America, he saw others copying his design, including Isaac Singer. He sued I. M. Singer & Co. for patent infringement and won. Singer had to pay Howe royalties on all the Singer sewing machines sold, and

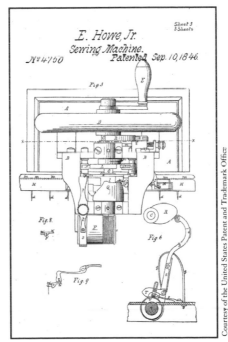

Courtesy of the United States Patent and Trademark Office

Patent No. US4750A for an improvement in sewing machines by Elias Howe

Howe died a rich man. Still, when you think of sewing machines, you think of Singer.

◀ ◀ ◀ **HOMEMADE STILTS** ▷ ▷ ▷

Please consult with an adult before using stilts; they could lead to falls and/or injury.

You'll need:

- 2 8-foot-long 2-x-4-inch boards (the type of wood used for framing houses)
- Ruler
- Pencil
- Handsaw
- Drill
- Screwdriver
- 4 3-inch lag bolts (or other strong fasteners) for the footrests
- Small metal handles and screws (optional)

To create:

1. Cut a 10-inch piece off each of the 8-foot pieces of wood. These 10-inch pieces will be your footrests.

2. Use your pencil to make a mark at the 12-inch point from one end of what remains of each of the 8-foot pieces of wood, which will be the main component of the stilts. (You want to be able to get on the stilts easily and reduce your chance

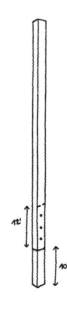

of falling while learning.
One foot for the height
of the footrests is the
recommended height for
beginners.)

3. Where you have marked the
12-inch point from the end
of each main piece of wood, drill
three holes on each stilt: one 1 inch
below your mark, another 4 inches
below that, and a third 4 inches
below that one. These are for the
lag bolts that will hold the footrests
(make sure you use a drill bit that is
slightly smaller than your lag-bolt
diameter). Screw three bolts securely
into each footrest, firmly attaching
it to the stilt. For safety, the footrests
must be securely attached. Test this
by having an adult stand on them.

4. For small hands, add metal handles
(attach them to the stilts using
screws).

5. Wear a bike helmet while using the
stilts, and practice on grass.

Times spent creating projects with other kids were some of the best times I had at school apart from being with the horses. They were the only times when I didn't get teased. I tried not to let it get to me, but sometimes I'd want to punch my tormentors. It wasn't only at school. I'd get teased in lots of places in public. I didn't look like other kids, didn't care about fashion or hairstyles. The boys called me "bones" because I was skinny and "workhorse" because I worked in the horse barn all the time. Teasing and bullying made the parking lot and cafeteria torture places. Bullying in high school made it the WORST period in my life.

The only time the teasing stopped was when I was doing an activity where I had a shared interest with other students. Activities such as horseback riding and building model rockets were a refuge from teasing. I was a big hit with the students the day I made a rocket that resembled our principal. Shared interests like Boy Scouts or Girl Scouts, electronics lab, or theater are great ways to be a part of something, especially for quirky and different kids. These activities are all about the shared goal. Something kind of amazing happened when we built our snowboard and flew down the hills of our New Hampshire boarding school, and when we took turns on our stilts, carrying on like we were circus clowns and giraffes and anything tall: no one teased me.

▷ ▷ ▷

THE WORD NERD

It may seem unbelievable, but the person who coined the term "nerd" was Dr. Seuss. In his 1950 book, *If I Ran the Zoo*, he has a line that describes the imaginary characters he would want for his zoo, "A Nerkle, a Nerd, and a SeerSucker, too." The nerd in the illustration looks more annoyed than nerdy; he doesn't have oversize glasses or a pocket protector. The term "geek" is a little older and originally comes from the sideshows of freaks in the early 1900s. It was a variant of the word "geck," which means dupe or fool. Somewhere along the way, the word "nerd" really took off to describe socially backward kids like me or anyone who was different. Only it has morphed in the last decade and a half, also referring to people who are supersmart STEM (which stands for Science, Technology, Engineering, and Mathematics) types like the scientists on *The Big Bang Theory*.

Make no mistake. I am a nerd. *Star Trek* was my favorite show when I was in high school. I could really relate to the logical Mr. Spock. In my career designing and building livestock systems, I worked with many quirky, brilliant millwrights. They could build anything. It may sound nerdy, but it was so much fun to sit in their job trailer and discuss how to build stuff.

The tides have turned for nerds, with the rise of Silicon

Valley and geniuses like Bill Gates, Steve Jobs, Steve Wozniak, and Mark Zuckerberg. Overnight, the kids who had spent many hours alone taking apart their computers and building new ones, or teaching themselves to code, were revolutionizing the world. Silicon Valley gave rise to nerd pride. If you ask me, the future is in the hands of the nerds, so be nice to us.

I was excited about making a wooden boat in sixth grade shop class, but I didn't know it would result in a lesson on the principle of displacement. In other words, why do boats float? The answer was discovered in a bathtub in ancient Greece, but for me the first challenge was making a seaworthy vessel. Our teacher supervised us handling the power jigsaw. It's a big deal when you advance from handheld tools to power tools, and you have to take a lot of precautions such as wearing safety goggles and special gloves and having adult supervision. We used one-inch-thick wooden boards and a boat-shaped flat board to form the bottom of the hull, which is the watertight body of the boat. The shop teacher cut out strips of pine on a power jigsaw to form the sides of the hull. Our job was to glue them together and smoothly shape the hull with sandpaper. Another way to easily smooth the glued-together sections is to use a tool called a spokeshave. It has two handles and a blade in the middle, similar to a plane. The tool is drawn over the surface of the wood. With the coping saw, I cut some quarter-inch plywood to form a deck; then I added a mast (the poles you fly the sails from) and cut a bedsheet for the sail. I glued my sail to the mast, but you can apply what you've learned about pulleys and make sails that can be hoisted up and down.

◄ ◄ ◄ **SAILBOAT** ▷ ▷ ▷

You'll need:

- Pencil
- 1 1¾-inch-thick, 2½-x-7-inch-long piece of softwood (such as balsa, pine, or alder wood)
- Coping saw or jigsaw
- Sandpaper (80 grit)
- Lightly dampened cloth
- Drill with ³⁄₈-inch bit
- 1 ¼-inch-thick, 8-inch-long dowel
- Scissors
- 6-inch square of craft canvas (for the sail)
- Wood glue
- 1 3-x-4-inch piece of ³⁄₈-inch-thick wood

To create:

1. Trace the shape of the bottom of a boat on your softwood (shown in the illustration) and cut out the shape with either a coping saw or a jigsaw. Sand the

rough surfaces. Make certain that you sand in the direction of the wood grain. Clean thoroughly with a lightly dampened cloth and let dry for half an hour.

2. Drill a hole in the softwood, about a third of the way back from the bow of the boat. Do not drill all the way through the wood.

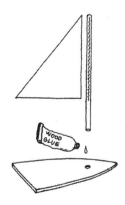

3. Place the dowel in the hole to make sure it fits tightly. Remove the dowel. Sand the boat and dowel to remove rough spots and make smooth to the touch. Again, clean thoroughly with a lightly dampened cloth and let dry.

4. Using scissors, cut a right-angle triangle out of the canvas to form the sail.

5. Starting at one end of the dowel, apply glue (in a straight line) to six inches of the dowel—the end with glue will be the top of the boat's mast. (Do not glue the bottom two inches of the dowel). Wrap the flat side of the canvas once around the

dowel (be sure to position the
canvas so that the right angle
of the triangle is toward the
bottom end of the dowel) and
press firmly to adhere. Place a
few drops of the glue into the
hole you have created for the
mast and set the bottom of the
dowel into the hole.

6. If your boat does not remain
    upright while you are sailing it, you can try
    weighting it down or creating a keel for the bottom
    of the boat out of a piece of wood board that is
    about 3 inches long, 4 inches tall (with an angle on
    one side if you can make it), and ³⁄₈ inch thick at
    its thickest, and then narrowed in the shape of a
    triangle so that it comes to a point at its tip. Place in
    the center underneath your sailboat by using wood
    glue to adhere the 3-inch side to the bottom of your
    boat with the thicker part facing the bow (front) and
    the narrower part facing the stern (back). Allow to
    dry thoroughly.

*Note: Your boat may still need additional weight on the
keel. If all else fails, tape a rock to the keel with duct tape.*

It was now time to try sailing my boat. There was a little brook that flowed under a bridge near our house. A friend and I rode to the bridge and parked our bikes. I could not wait to sail my boat in the brook, and with much anticipation I placed it in the water. It immediately tipped over. It was a total failure. I was very disappointed that the boat I had worked on for so long was not seaworthy.

I went back to school and asked the shop teacher why my boat had tipped over. He explained that it needed a keel to hold it upright. A keel is a flat blade, kind of like a shark fin, that is attached to the bottom of a sailboat. When submerged in the water, the keel helps keep the boat from being blown sideways. Our boats never got keels because the school

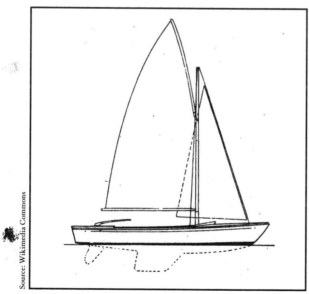

Source: Wikimedia Commons

Boat's keel

shop had no capabilities for metalwork, but I was satisfied with learning why it had tipped over. I realize now that I could also have weighted down my boat with rocks to keep it from tipping. Or I could have fastened brackets to it or tied on fishing sinkers. You might think that adding weight would make something sink. There is, however, a reason why boats that weigh fifty tons don't sink or tip over. You will better understand these principles after you experiment with floating paper cups and various types of glasses in your sink.

WHATEVER FLOATS YOUR BOAT

Archimedes is a big deal. We already know that he gets credit for explaining leverage. But the principle named after him (Archimedes' principle) has to do with water displacement. The ruler of Syracuse didn't trust his goldsmith and asked Archimedes to determine whether his crown was 100 percent gold. The catch was that Archimedes couldn't harm the crown in any way, such as, for instance, by sawing through it or chipping off a piece to analyze the gold content. Archimedes contemplated this dilemma. The answer came when he was getting into a full bathtub and observed the water rising. You have probably observed this yourself. He realized that the amount of water he had displaced by getting into the tub was the same as the volume of his own body. (Volume is the amount of space a thing takes up—in this case, Archimedes' body in the tub.)

Archimedes submerged the king's crown in water to

determine the volume of the crown. He then did the same with a lump of pure gold that weighed the same as the crown. When he compared the amount of water displaced by the crown and the gold, he found that the crown had a greater volume and therefore must have been mixed with silver or some lighter base metal. As the story goes, the goldsmith was beheaded, and the world received a law of science that explains buoyancy and displacement.

I recently tried some of my own experiments that involved displacement and buoyancy. I filled a sink with water, and when I pushed an empty paper cup down into the water, I could feel the "upward buoyant force" that would float a boat. When I let go of the cup, it floated and immediately tipped over. Weighting the floating cup with added water did not prevent it from tipping over. My childhood boat was like the paper cup. I was more successful with two glasses that I tried. The best glass had a heavy base. I set it on the bottom of an empty sink. When I filled the sink with water, it magically lifted up and floated like a boat without tipping. Another water glass also worked after I added some water to it. The heavy glass base provided ballast, which stabilized and prevented tipping. You should carefully experiment with different types of glasses to find the ones that will float like boats without tipping.

Or you can test some other objects around the house to see if they float. Try an apple. Cut it in half, carve out the center, and see if it floats or tips. Add a few marbles. Does it steady itself? Add a few more. See what happens. We spent an entire science class predicting what things around our classroom would sink or float, but it didn't occur to me then that adding weight to my boat would have stabilized it so it could float. Now, of course, I understand that it isn't weight alone but the distribution of weight and the displacement of water that make things buoyant.

SEAWORTHY

Maria A. Beasley was that rare thing: a successful inventor and businesswoman in the 1800s. In 1882, she received a patent for the Life-Raft. According to her patent claim, "The object of my invention is to furnish a fire-proof, compact, safe and readily-launched raft, which can be made instantly available when required." Until then, rafts had basically been made of planks of wood. Beasley added a railing guard to her raft that could easily fold up and that was buoyed by hollow metallic floats. She received fifteen other patents for a wide variety of inventions including foot warmers, an anti-derailment device for trains, a steam generator, and the invention that made her a wealthy woman: the barrel-hoop driving machine. Here, too, she claims, "The object of my invention is to construct

a machine to do what manual labor is now employed to do."
Today, we hear a lot about robots eventually taking away jobs
from people—but it's been going on for centuries, whenever
new technologies are developed. Some people applaud progress,
other resist it. Beasley's machine was used to force iron hoops
onto barrels, making them strong enough to hold their contents securely for a long time. These barrels were used for food
and wine storage, and Beasley earned approximately $20,000 a
year (at a time when women generally earned $3 a day).

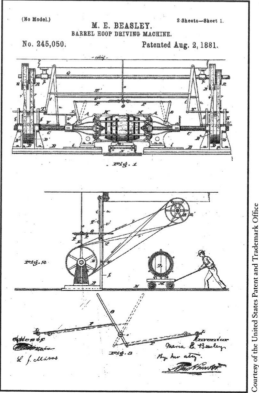

*Patent No. US245050A for a barrel-hoop
driving machine by Maria Beasley*

Another project I loved to make that used wood *and* had moving parts was marionettes. A marionette is like a jumping-jack puppet, except there is no leverage involved. Instead, you manipulate each appendage individually. You can probably guess that my favorite part was the mechanics of making them work. What's fun about assembling and using marionettes is getting good at manipulating all the limbs. The strings are attached to a crossbar, which can be as simple as two Popsicle sticks glued into a cross, or as complex as a frame with a hand handle, or a body handle. One crossbar controls the arms, and the other crossbar controls the body.

The easiest way to put a marionette together is with a pack of puppet body parts that you can get at a crafts store. Usually these come assembled with little eyelets to thread the string through. We used blocks of wood, which we connected with strips of fabric that we stapled into the wood with a staple gun.

◁ ◁ ◁ **MARIONETTE** ▷ ▷ ▷

You'll need:

- Pencil
- White poster board
- Scissors
- 6 paper fasteners
- 2 pencil-thin dowels (one 6 inches long and one 9 inches long), or use pencils

- Extra-strength packing tape
- 4 8-to-12-inch-long pieces of heavy string
- 1 3-to-5-inch-long piece of heavy string

To create:

1. Draw a torso, a head, two arms, and two legs on the poster board. Each body part should be separate but proportional, and the finished product should be about 10 inches long.

2. Cut out the body pieces with your scissors.

3. Place the pieces of your marionette on a flat surface. Place the legs and arms so that they overlap the torso slightly (about ¼ inch). Using the point of your scissors, make a hole in each spot where the joints overlap.

4. Insert a paper fastener into each of the holes you have created. You should be able to freely and easily move the joints.

5. Create the "handle" by making a cross from the two dowels. Tape the dowels together at the center where the two pieces intersect.

6. Make four holes in your marionette—one above each knee and one at each of the wrists. Also make a hole at the top of the head. Attach a length of string to each hole and tie each one to a branch of the handle. Tie the string attached to the head to the center of the cross. Twist and turn the handle to watch your marionette dance!

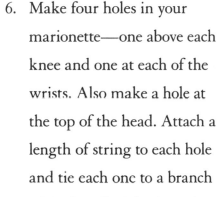

Sometimes we'd make the heads of our marionettes out of papier-mâché. You can also use Styrofoam or corrugated cardboard, though marionettes work better with more weight so the arms or legs will drop back down after you've made them move. You can always weigh them down with their clothes, too. Keeping the strings from tangling is the hard part. If you start with shorter strings you'll have less tangling, but you won't be able to make the puppet move all that much. Once you get the hang of using the crossbar and manipulating the string, you can lengthen the strings.

◄ ◄ ◄ PAPIER-MÂCHÉ PUPPET HEAD ▷ ▷ ▷

You'll need:

- Warm water
- Flour
- Bowl
- Metal spoon or whisk
- Balloon or Styrofoam ball and dowel
- Milk carton
- Scissors
- Newspapers
- Tempera or acrylic paint
- Paintbrushes
- Miscellaneous items for decorating (example: yarn for hair, ribbon, beads, buttons)
- Glue

To create:

1. The simplest way to make papier-mâché paste is to mix 5 parts water with 1 part flour in a bowl. Stir to get the lumps out and keep adding water if the mixture gets too thick.

2. Blow up your balloon or put your

Styrofoam ball on a dowel. Cut the bottom of a milk carton or improvise to make a base that the balloon or ball can stand up in.

3. Cut or tear the newspaper into approximately 30 1-x-3-inch strips.

4. Dip the first strip into the paste and pull it gently between two fingers to remove excess paste. You don't want the puppet head to be too soggy. Smoothly layer the strip on the balloon (this will make it easier to paint and decorate). Continue with the next strip and the next until you have at least 3 layers of strips covering the balloon.

5. Allow to dry overnight. The puppet head must be completely dry before you begin painting.

6. Paint the facial features. Allow to dry.

7. Use glue to adhere yarn for the hair. Then embellish the rest of the face and head. Remember to glue a yarn loop at the top of the head.

I figured marionettes had already been around for too long to be patented, but I found a few patents from the 1930s and 1940s that claim small modifications, including one that has a movable jaw and one that is supposed to move in a "natural manner." I also found a patent for something called an Invisible Marionette, which is literally just feet that look like they have been sawed off a body, and is one of the freakiest things I've ever seen.

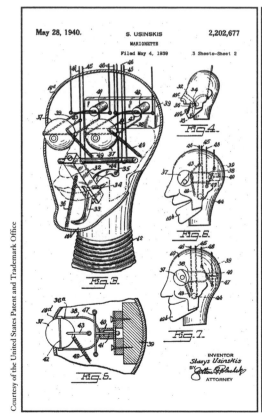
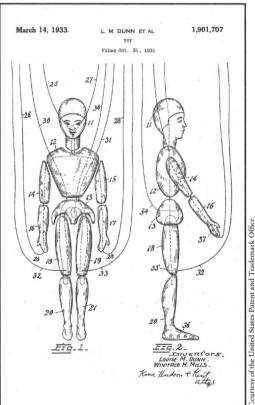

Patent No. US2202677A for a marionette with a movable jaw by Stasys Usinskis

Patent No. US1901707A for a marionette toy that moves in a natural manner by Louise M. Dunn and Winifred H. Mills

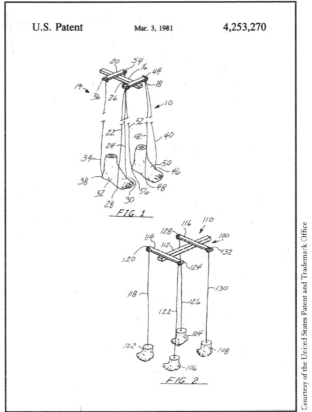

Patent No. US4253270A for an invisible marionette
by Carl E. Elwing and Mary J. Elwing

PAPER CHASE

....

The stapler is a good example of an invention that evolved

over time and through the hands and minds of different inven-

tors. First consider this: staples didn't exist until paper was

invented. It may seem obvious, but I think that's an exciting fact because it means that when humans invent something new, there is a domino effect as many more new inventions will be created as a result. People date the first stapler back to the French King Louis XV, who needed to secure his court documents. French toolmakers came up with the first staple, which was used one at a time, was made of gold, and had the royal court's insignia on it.

In 1866, inventor George McGill made the first commercially successful stapler, which was known as a "bendable paper fastener." It looked like a sewing machine and punched the staple through paper, but each staple still had to be loaded in one at a time. Then, in 1877, Henry R. Heyl received a patent for his improvement, which could both send the staple through the paper and bend the wire up underneath to cinch it. The next truly exciting innovation for the stapler came in 1895 when Eli Hotchkiss introduced the strip of staples wired together that got inserted into the body of the stapler, which enabled continuous stapling. It may not sound like much, but until then, remember every staple was inserted manually and punched through the paper one at a time. Staple strips are still used today, but they are now glued together. Hotchkiss made a few other design improvements, and this stapler, named the No. 1 Automatic Paper Fastener, remained the most popular for forty years. But there was still one little problem: loading the staples in an efficient way.

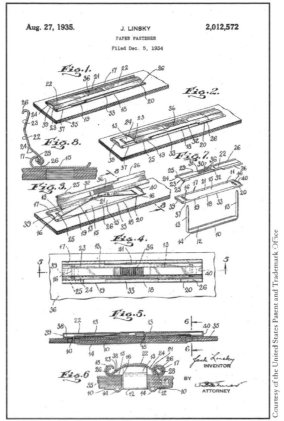

Patent No. US2012572A for a paper fastener
by Jack Linsky

When Russian immigrant Jack Linsky was fourteen years old, he worked as a delivery boy for a stationery company on the Lower East Side of New York. At nineteen, he opened his own stationery wholesale store. When he couldn't find a stapler that worked well, he invented one of his own. In 1939, Linsky made one modification that changed the way staplers work: he opened up the top of the stapler so the staples could be easily loaded top down into the body of the stapler. His wife, Belle, named the stapler Swingline, and it's still the most popular stapler on the market. You might even have one at home— open it up, and you'll see the whole history of the stapler.

One of the reasons I loved working with wood was that I could do so many things with it: build with it, float it, warp it, staple fabric into it, paint it, and make just about anything with it. Look around in the garage, or go to a lumberyard, where they might be happy to give you a bag of wood scraps. That's what I used to do, and it's part of how I became an equipment designer, though back then I thought I was just having fun.

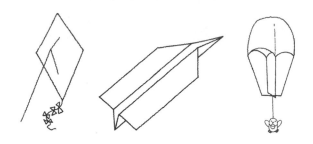

• CHAPTER FOUR •

THINGS THAT FLY

I was by myself, flying home from my aunt's ranch the summer after my senior year of high school and right before going to college. The plane was a 707 jet, American Airlines, and I was seated toward the back. Those were the days when you got dressed up to fly on a plane. I still remember using the headset, which looked like a doctor's stethoscope. I was happily listening to music, watching the stewardess work her way down the aisle with trays of food. Just then, the plane lurched to the side and the trays flew up to the ceiling. The stewardesses were screaming for us to put our safety belts on. The next thing they told us was, "Emergency landing! Emergency landing!" I had one thought: I'm going to die. Then a second thought: what a waste of my life.

The plane landed in Salina, Kansas, on an old army base. It was fishtailing down the runway, and we were told to evacuate down the slide and not to stop running after we hit the ground. I couldn't believe it. Just an hour ago, I was reading the safety card and wondering what it would be like to go down the slides. Police cars and bomb squads were swarming the plane. It turned out that a woman had told a fellow passenger that a bomb in her suitcase was going to blow up in ten minutes. He told the pilot and that set the emergency evacuation in motion. No bomb was found as far as I know, and we were eventually put on another plane home. All our stuff had been dumped in a huge pile and searched by the bomb squad. I had two of my prized possessions in there, my Instamatic camera and my Polaroid Swinger, and fortunately I found them among the wallets and keys and handkerchiefs and all the other stuff people cram into their bags.

For a long time after that experience, I "white-knuckled" every plane trip I went on; now, I fly all over the world and never think about it. The way I got over my fear of flying was to learn more about how airplanes worked. This made them less scary. I learned that the wings are designed to flex and that they will not break off. Airplanes went from frightening to fascinating. My fear of flying ended after I had the opportunity to fly in the cockpit of an ancient Constellation airplane that transported dairy cows to Puerto Rico. After we returned to Miami, I discovered that cow pee was dripping through holes drilled in the bottom of the fuselage. Planes could be abused and they still flew.

My very first plane trip was uneventful, except my ears were killing me the whole time. It was a Lockheed Electra prop plane.

I was in the sixth grade and we were on a family trip to Canada. What I remember most clearly was the moment when the plane broke through the clouds and we were flying above them. I had never seen the tops of clouds. I thought that was pretty wonderful.

I always loved watching things in the sky. As I've said, anything visually stimulating caught my attention: birds, kites, planes. And I loved making anything that could fly. Model airplanes never much interested me because after you put them together, they just sat there. I didn't have any patience for that. If it wasn't aerodynamic, I didn't see the point.

I made my first kite when I was around seven. For the body, I used the paper that comes on the inside of a round cookie tin. If you've ever seen one, you know that it's sort of quilted and a little waxy, thinner than cardboard and also lighter. I attached some string to it and tied it to the back of my tricycle. It didn't work all that great, and that's when I got it into my head to make a bird kite.

Source: ABC Television via Wikimedia Commons

The Flying Nun with her downward-pointing wings

I tipped the sides of the wings up, which is something I had seen my father do with a paper plane. It made sense to me even though I didn't yet understand the reason why. When I was in college there was a popular TV show called *The Flying Nun*. By then I knew that the aerodynamics were off because the wings on the Flying Nun's wimple were pointed down.

◁ ◁ ◁ MY CHILDHOOD BIRD KITE ▷ ▷ ▷

You'll need:

- Scissors
- 1 letter-size (11½-x-8¾-inch) pocketless folder
- Marker
- Ruler
- Scotch tape
- Cotton thread
- Crepe paper party streamers (1¾ inch width)

To create:

1. Using scissors, cut your file folder in half. Each half can be made into its own kite!

2. Use your marker to make a dot in the middle of one of the long sides of the folder, right at its edge. This is now the bottom of your kite. Place another two dots on the edge of each of the short sides of the folder 6¼ inches up

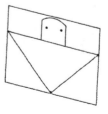

from the bottom. Draw three lines between the three dots so that you have one big triangle.

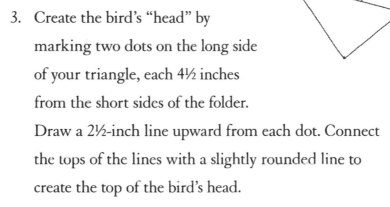

3. Create the bird's "head" by marking two dots on the long side of your triangle, each 4½ inches from the short sides of the folder. Draw a 2½-inch line upward from each dot. Connect the tops of the lines with a slightly rounded line to create the top of the bird's head.

4. Using scissors, cut out the bird shape.

5. Fold the wing tips up by 90 degrees, 1 inch from the ends of the wings.

6. With a small piece of tape, fasten a 10-foot length of thread to the head. (When I was a kid, I attached this string to the back of my bike to fly my kite, but you can also run with it and even make this string longer!)

7. Attach an 18-inch length of thread to the rear of the kite. Try experimenting with the length of this thread.

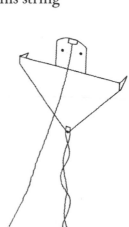

8. Attach a 22-inch length of the crepe paper party streamer to the end of the thread at the rear of the kite. Try

experimenting with the length of the crepe paper. Try different tail materials.

9. Bend the bird's head down slightly. This helps provide lift. Experiment with the angle of the head until you get the lift you want. Your bird kite is now ready to sail away!

Note: You may have to experiment to get it to work. The textured heavy art paper that I used as a child is not readily available, so I had to use file folders instead this time around. They have a smooth surface that may have an effect on flight characteristics.

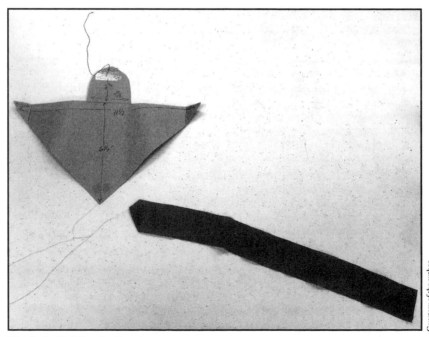

This is the bird kite that I made.

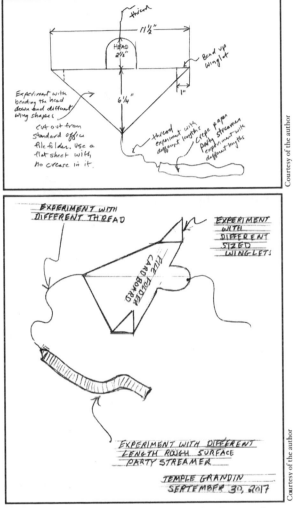

My schematics of my bird kite that I drew when I recreated my childhood project (flat view and perspective drawing)

For things to fly, there are two forces at work: lift and drag. In a *Scientific American* article, Tom Veilleux, a senior scientist, and Vince Simonds, a director of aerodynamic research at the Top-Flite golf company, provide a good way to think about how it works: "Holding your arm out of the window of a moving car easily illustrates this phenomenon . . . Drag acts to directly oppose motion, whereas lift acts in a direction perpendicular to motion. As you rotate your hand in the air stream, you vary the amount and direction of the lift and drag acting on your hand." So when a jet is lifting off the ground, there is a certain amount of drag as it pushes against the air; the winglets reduce drag by redirecting the flow of air (and they also conserve fuel). When I tilted up the ends of my kite, I was just copying my dad's paper plane, but it worked on my bird kite, which had a totally different design. It may sound really simple, but it's how most inventions start: by observation. The inventor thinks: Is there something I can improve? Something I can refine? Something I can transform, or possibly create?

WHAT A DRAG

....

Richard Whitcomb's (1921–2009) life is a perfect example of a childhood passion becoming a lifelong calling. He had

Source: NASA on The Commons @ Flickr Commons

Richard Whitcomb

been fascinated with planes from a young age, making models and flying them in competitions. He went to college for aeronautical engineering and then went to work in the wind tunnels at Langley, a research center run by the National Advisory Committee for Aeronautics, which became NASA. Whitcomb had been working on the challenge of reducing drag, which enabled the plane to go faster while saving fuel at the same time. He vividly recalls when he had his first eureka! moment: tapering the body of the plane like the shape of a Coke bottle

Source: United States Department of Energy via Wikimedia Commons

An old Coke bottle

to reduce drag. In a NASA video remembering Whitcomb's life, he explains how it happened: "I had the idea. Then we built some models to try and demonstrate it. We built airplanes with Coke bottle shape fuselages and lo and behold the drag on the wing just disappeared. Now there was when I was really thrilled . . . It worked perfectly. It was not some oddball theory. It was a practical means of reducing drag." Another significant contribution to reducing drag happened when Whitcomb observed the tipped-up ends of bird wings. They gave him the idea for winglets.

Tom Crouch, fellow NASA colleague, said, "Dick Whitcomb's intellectual fingerprints are on virtually every commercial aircraft flying today." I think that is the coolest, when something you create lives beyond you. Another colleague said Whitcomb had the two most important qualities in an inventor: tenacity and perseverance, spending a decade on each of his inventions. He received many awards in his life, including the National

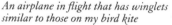
An airplane in flight that has winglets similar to those on my bird kite

A bird in flight

Medal of Science. And his picture is included among those of aerodynamic titans like the Wright brothers, Amelia Earhart, Charles Lindbergh, and John Glenn at the Wright Brothers National Memorial. When he died, his ashes were scattered by plane over the Chesapeake Bay.

If you meet an inventor, the best question you can ask, or at least one great question, is: where did you get your idea? For Whitcomb, a Coke bottle and a bird are part of the story.

After adding winglets, I decided to put a tail on my kite, which was something I had also observed when watching other children flying kites. I found some crepe paper streamers from a birthday party and attached them to the kite with string and tape. I was always rummaging around for materials to use in my experiments:

typing paper, cardboard, string, cloth from our rag drawer, acorns, twigs, those funny double wings that fall from maple trees that we used to stick on our noses. (I later learned they are pods carrying seeds for the tree to reproduce.) With party streamers attached, the kite flew behind my trike about six feet in the air, and I was pretty proud of myself.

Re-creating my kites as an adult, however, required more work than I expected. First I used lightweight plastic strips from a grocery bag for the tail. They worked so poorly that I drove across town to get the exact same crepe paper party streamers I had used as a kid. I was curious to see if the crepe paper party streamers would make a difference—they did, but it wasn't for the reason I had imagined. I thought they worked because they were lighter, but in fact, it was the rough surface of the paper. It's counterintuitive. You would think that light and smooth paper would fly more easily, but it's the texture of the paper that has a positive effect on its flight characteristics.

Take early golf balls for example. Originally, they were completely smooth. Then golfers observed that old beat-up balls with rough surfaces tended to fly farther than new balls. They didn't know why a smooth golf ball would travel a shorter distance than a nicked ball, but it turned out there was scientific evidence that proved them right. Tom Veilleux and Vince Simonds also study the launch angle and spin rate of golf balls. As scientists, they analyze how the dimples create the tiny pockets of air that give the ball more lift. Researchers have found that a dimpled ball is quieter as it passes through the air. A non-smooth shape also makes a jet exhaust quieter due to reducing turbulence. It's the same principle. Look at this Boeing Aircraft patent. It shows a scalloped exhaust. Creating pockets of air affects aerodynamics and acoustics. I'm sure the engineers at Boeing tested all different patterns on the exhausts in the wind tunnels before coming up with the scalloped exhaust of the 2011 Dreamliner. Something as seemingly small and insignificant as a dimple on a golf ball can make a huge difference in design, and a little scalloped groove can get a patent.

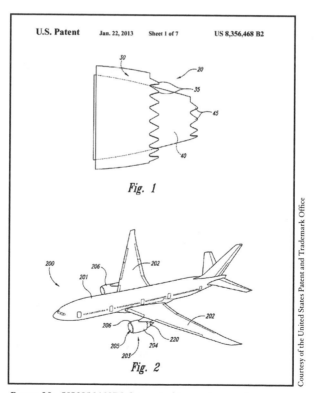

Patent No. US8356468B2 for gas turbine engine nozzle configurations by David F. Cerra

HOW THE GOLF BALL GOT ITS DIMPLES

According to Rain Noe, senior editor of Core77, a design website, the first golf balls were made of beech wood, and they weren't perfectly round. In the seventeenth century, golf balls known as Fetheries were made of leather stuffed with goose feathers, and stitched shut (I'm guessing like a softball). In the mid 1800s, Reverend Adam Paterson noticed that a package used a rubbery substance to keep the contents safe. He heated the material and injected it into a round mold and let it harden, creating the first molded ball. They were called "gutties," named for the "gutta-percha" sap from the sapodilla tree. They were the first mass-manufactured golf ball. This is when golfers first noticed that dented gutties tended to fly farther than new ones. A popular ball at the time was called the Agrippa because golfers thought the head of the golf club could get a better grip on a pimply surface. The Musselburgh golf ball added another variation to the surface with a grid-like effect.

Another accidental discovery was made when Coburn Haskell was waiting for his friend Bertram Work at the B. F. Goodrich factory (the story goes they were going for a game of golf). While waiting for his friend, Haskell started winding rubber threads into a ball shape and observed how high it bounced. In 1899, the two men patented their invention, citing their ball as having lightness and durability, and as being highly resilient under strong impact. You can see on the patent illustrations how the center is made of rubber thread wound around a core. Drawing #4 on the patent actually looks like a ball of yarn or a rubber-band ball. These balls were cheaper than the gutties, flew farther, and increased the popularity of golf. Then in 1909, golf ball manufacturer and engineer William Taylor, having observed players purposefully nick their golf

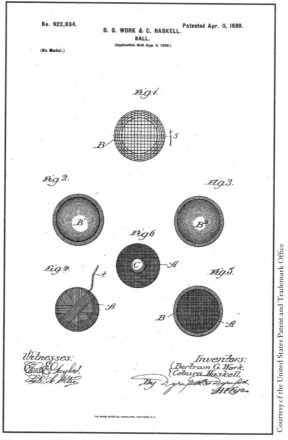

Patent No. US622834A for a golf ball by Bertram Work and Coburn Haskell

balls, began to dimple the balls he produced, and marketed them as the Spalding "Glory" Dimple Golf Ball. One hundred years later, no one has changed that design, though improvements to golf ball physics are always being tested with different urethane skins and synthetic resin cores. That's how golf balls got their dimples.

The first kites were made in China from silk and bamboo. They were used to send military messages and measure the wind. Kites eventually made their way to Europe and America. The most famous story involving a kite, as you probably know, is when Benjamin Franklin discovered electricity. He tied a metal key to a string and flew it during an electrical storm. (Do not try this at home!) He was lucky he wasn't killed because a few scientists in Europe, trying to replicate the experiment, were. Franklin was the first to show that there are two kinds of electrical charges, positive and negative, and how electrons travel between entities of different electrical potential. This became the basis of our knowledge of electricity.

GO FLY A KITE

According to the Nebraska State Historical Society, kites were involved in the construction of the bridge that connected the United States and Canada over the great gorge known as Niagara Falls. Charles Ellet Jr. was hired as the engineer. He chose the narrowest point over the falls to build the bridge. Ellet had experience with suspension bridges and knew that the first challenge was getting an initial line across the body of water. Once that is accomplished, rope, cable, and stronger materials can be extended to form the basis of the bridge. Between the great expanse of 800 feet from cliff to cliff over the falls and the 225-foot drop, the chance of getting across seemed impossible. Ellet thought of using a rocket; another idea was shooting a bombshell from a canon.

Then, in January 1948, a local ironworker suggested a kite-flying contest to get the line across the water. The prize

Source: Wikimedia Commons

Charles Ellet Jr.

was $5 or $10 (sources differ), but would be about $135 today. Lots of people turned out with their kites. The Canadian side was deemed best for launching kites because the winds blew from west to east. A fifteen-year-old American boy named Homan Walsh from upstate New York took a ferry to the Canadian side and flew his kite, called Union. He waited a whole day for a good wind. His first attempt failed when the string broke on the rocks and ice. It was his third attempt that proved victorious when the string of his kite made the connection from one side to the other. The bridge could at last be built thanks to a fifteen-year-old and his kite.

My siblings and I used to fly all kind of kites when we were kids. You can still buy them pretty cheaply, but they're more fun to design and make, experimenting with different shapes, fabrics, plastic, crossbars, tails, and strings. In high school, I'm not sure what possessed me, but I made a six-foot kite, which I named Out to Lunch and flew with clothesline. It's fun to see how big you can make something. (It's also fun to make miniatures.) As with my snowboard and stilts, the materials were largely "found" around campus and construction sites. The crossbars were made of thin strips of wood; the material for the kite was the heavy brown paper that paneling came packaged in. For the perimeter, I used baling twine, which we used in the barn to tie up the baled hay. I stapled the brown paper to the frame and folded it over the baling twine and stapled that, too. For a tail, I used more baling twine and rags. I used trial and error to figure out how many rags were needed. Attaching a tail to a kite requires applying the principles of drag and lift. Without a tail, the kite will be unstable and will probably nose-dive just as soon as you get it off the ground.

◁ ◁ ◁ **KITE** ▷ ▷ ▷

You'll need:

- Scissors

- 1 heavy-duty trash bag

- 1 21-inch-long, $^3/_{16}$-inch-thick wooden dowel

- Ruler

- 1 14-inch-long, $^3/_{16}$-inch-thick wooden dowel

- 1 full roll of 10-ply cotton string

- Duct tape

- Crepe paper (like I used on my childhood kite)

To create:

1. Cut the trash bag open and lay it on the floor or on a table.

2. On the 21-inch dowel, make a mark at the 12-inch point (from the top) and position the 14-inch dowel there to form a cross. Secure the cross firmly with string. This will provide the framework for your kite.

3. Place the cross in the very center of the open trash bag. The top of the cross should be even with the very

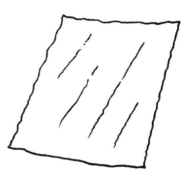

top of your bag. Tape all the dowels
to the trash bag with duct tape.

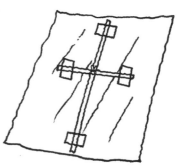

4. Starting at the top right, fold
   the top edges of the trash bag
   inward in ½-inch increments.
   Tape the edges down. Repeat
   with the same number of
   folds on the other three sides
   of the kite. A diamond shape should
   immediately begin to appear.

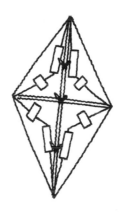

5. With your scissors, punch a hole in the
   center of the bag next to the dowel
   and about 6 inches from the top.
   Punch another hole 8 inches from
   the bottom of the kite, also in the
   center next to the dowel.

6. Thread one 12-inch piece of string through
   those two holes so that the string hangs on
   the side without the dowels, and secure the
   string firmly on the dowels. Tie your roll
   of string to the very center of that string.

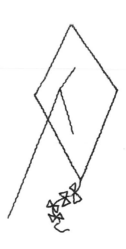

7. Turn your kite over. Create a tail from
   ribbon and/or crepe paper and fasten it
   securely onto the lower portion of the
   dowel in the back. The crepe paper

will need to be taped securely on. Your kite is now ready to sail away!

Note: Kites will often fly better if the horizontal crossbar is bowed slightly. This can be accomplished by bending the crossbar and keeping it in a bowed position with a piece of string. It will look like the bow for a bow and arrow. Be careful not to break the crossbar.

Note: Kites work best if the string you're using to fly the kite has more than one attachment point. This is called a bridle. When the bridle is designed properly, the kite will fly on an angle. Experiment with different lengths and angles of the bridle. You can also experiment with different tails and with the shape of the kite.

I took Out to Lunch to the nearest hill. I can still remember holding on to the clothesline with two hands while it whipped in the wind. Fresh off my victory, I planned to make a ten-foot kite for my next project. The only change in design was the use of wallpaper to cover the kite. It got off the ground, and my heart soared the way it does when anything lifts off, only then it took a sharp turn sideways, busted in midair, and came crashing down.

The first planes I ever flew were made of paper. We didn't need any fancy equipment or tools, and the results were satisfying. A simple paper airplane can teach you a lot. I'm sure you remember the first time you made a plane and watched it crash. You learn pretty quickly through trial and error how you have to taper the front of the plane into a point. I can still remember the happy feeling of watching something I made fly.

◁ ◁ ◁ SIMPLE PAPER AIRPLANE ▷ ▷ ▷

You'll need:

- 1 sheet of 8½-x-11-inch paper
- Ruler (optional: use to create flatter and sharper creases)

To create:

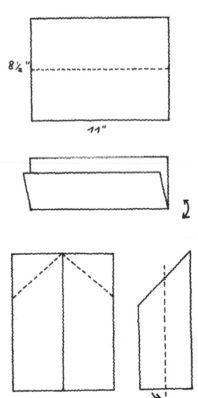

1. Fold your paper in half lengthwise and then unfold.

2. Holding your paper upright, so the shorter side is up, fold both of the top corners down to the middle crease.

3. Once the corners are folded, fold the paper in half again lengthwise so that the folded-down corners are on the inside of the folded paper. Then take

each of the two unfolded
long edges of the paper and
fold each one down so that
the unfolded edge of the
paper meets the folded edge.

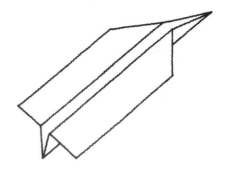

4. If your plane has a tendency
   to nose-dive, bend the tail
   edge up slightly. It will fly
   better at slower speeds.

◁ ◁ ◁ COMPLEX PAPER AIRPLANE ▷ ▷ ▷

You'll need:

- 1 sheet of 8½-x-11-inch paper
- Ruler (optional: use to create flatter and sharper
  creases)

To create:

1. Fold your paper in half
   lengthwise and then unfold.
2. Holding your paper upright, so
   the shorter side is up, fold both
   of the top corners down to the
   middle crease.

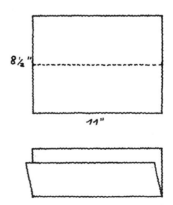

3. Then fold the left side down to the center crease and repeat with the right side.

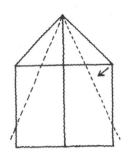

4. Fold the left side over to the right side and then fold each side out and down so that it lines up with the middle crease. This plane is very aerodynamic because of the sleekness and will have less drag because of its narrow wings. This plane will fly fast!

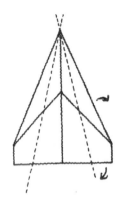

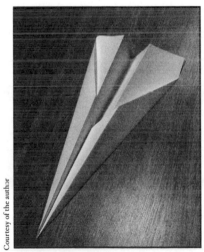

Courtesy of the author

This is a complex paper airplane that I made out of printer paper

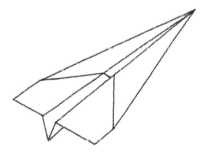

Note: Try folding single pieces of printer paper in every way you can think of and see which kinds of shapes fly best.

The next plane I put together was made from balsa wood and came in a kit that I got at Woolworth. It cost 69¢, which was two weeks' allowance. Sometimes I'd buy the small one for 39¢ and use the leftover change for comic books. The brand name was Guillow's, a company that was started in 1926. Paul Guillow was a retired World War I pilot who started out by producing his planes in the barn of his family's backyard. The following year, Charles Lindbergh made his famous transatlantic flight from New York to Paris in his *Spirit of St. Louis*. The country went crazy for everything pertaining to aviation.

I really loved my little plane and ran my own flight tests over and over, launching it from different heights, adjusting the placement of the wings, taking it out on windy days, basically experimenting with every different flight scenario. When I recently went to my local hobby shop to find a plane, I was delighted to see that Guillow's was still making them. Only when I got it home, I was a little disappointed. The red plastic propeller seemed smaller and lighter to me. The pieces were a little less sturdy. Still, I was eager to assemble the glider. There were only four steps:

1. Press the rudder and stabilizer into the slots on the body.
2. Slide the wing through the slot in the body and
   center it.
3. Attach the plastic propeller over the front of the body.
4. Hook up the rubber band.

Then you turn the propeller clockwise until the rubber band twists like a length of licorice, and you launch it from your hand. The directions on the plastic sleeve it comes in suggest moving the wings farther up or down if the plane nose-dives or stalls midair. You could also move the wings to the right or left to correct nose-dives to either side. When I was a kid, I just loved tinkering, making every adjustment possible just to see what happened.

My childhood Guillow's plane would fly six to eight feet off the ground after it had taken off from our driveway. Now when I assembled the plane, it barely got off the ground. When I tried the road outside my condo for a runway it crashed into the curb. I tried moving the wings, sliding them up and down, right and left, but the plane only cleared a few inches.

TRIAL AND ERROR

In 1844, American inventor Charles Goodyear was granted a patent for "improvement in India-rubber fabrics." This improvement was a process called "vulcanizing," named for the Roman god of fire, Vulcan. What it boiled down to was making natural rubber products more malleable so that they wouldn't either melt in too hot temperatures or crack in the cold. Though Goodyear had no knowledge of chemistry, he unlocked the molecular structure of rubber. He began experimenting at home at the age of thirty-three after a series of financial setbacks (including being jailed for debts). Stories

Source: Library of Congress

Charles Goodyear

vary, but the discovery was made when Goodyear accidentally left raw rubber, sulfur, and lead together on a stove. Heated, they created a substance that could be molded. It took another five years before he perfected the material. Then, in 1844, with his newly minted patent in hand, he found manufacturers who saw the value of Goodyear's process for their goods, including shoes, pencil erasers, life jackets, balls, hats, and rafts. Eventually, the material would be used for roofs, floors, assembly lines, shock absorbers, and tires. His discovery changed the industrial world, but when Goodyear died he left his family in debt after lengthy court battles over his patents wiped them out financially. Sometimes even a patent can't protect you.

The Goodyear Tire & Rubber Company, founded in 1898, is respectfully named after Charles Goodyear, though there is no relation. A man named Frank Seiberling, an inventor in his own right, borrowed $3,500 from his brother-in-law to start the company with his brother Charles. Among his many patents for improving the safety and performance of his tires, Seiberling invented a machine to make the tires, which until then had been made by hand. In the time it took for five tires to be built by hand, Seiberling's machine could produce sixty. What's remarkable about the design of his patent is that it uses a series of rollers to

Frank Seiberling

Source: Wikimedia Commons

produce continuous strips of rubber, much the same way Louis Nicolas Robert produced his continuous paper. The Goodyear Company is still around today, over 119 years later. In 2016, the company sold 166.1 million tires!

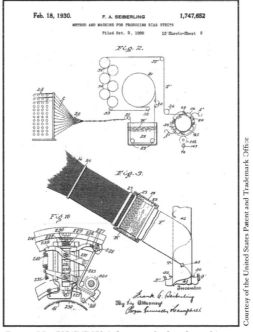

Courtesy of the United States Patent and Trademark Office

Patent No. US1747652A for a method and machine for producing bias strips by Frank Seiberling

The trial and error involved in placing the wings on my plane would have been good early training if I had decided to be a pilot. My testing wasn't so different from what airplane simulators do; they give pilots hands-on experience navigating planes under many different conditions. You might have played a flight simulator video game where it was fun to shoot missiles and explode things and navigate. The problem comes when your plane goes down and you have no idea how to fix it. One thing I know for sure: all the engineers and mechanical engineers I work with know how to fix things because they work with their hands. What if your only experience of a plane came from a video game or from simulators? I think video games are fun, but up to a point. There are studies that blame video games for everything from teen depression to encouraging violence. But there are also studies that suggest video games improve hand–eye coordination, reaction time, motor skills, and memory. Either way, they don't take the place of hands-on experience. When I get called to a job because something is not working, I have to be able to understand the design *and* work on the equipment. It's not enough to draft pretty designs if you don't know how they work.

When I first started working on my cattle-handling systems, I must have toured twenty-five facilities to see what they were doing right and what they were doing wrong. That's called "bottom-up" surveying. It's an important first step, because you don't want to reinvent the wheel if there is a good system or method in place that can be used as a model. My job was to find a solution to the cattle not wanting to move through the chutes. One of the very first things I noticed that slowed the flow of animals was the contrast of light and dark caused by shadows cast by the bars on a fence. Other times it was rapid movement, like a flag waving nearby. Even things as seemingly insignificant as a piece of plastic caught on a fence, a hose on the ground, a change from concrete to metal on the ground surface, a shiny reflection on a vehicle, or a puddle could impede their process.

A cattle feed yard that I visited early in my career. I observed that the cattle would balk at shadows and sun stripes.

I was able to figure this out because my own nervous system is a lot like that of the animals I work with. I'm highly sensitive to sensory experiences, and changes in the environment used to really set me off as a child. The same with the cattle: anything new or novel could make them fearful. I highly encourage all kids, parents, and teachers to see children's sensitivities as strengths, because that's what they are. When I was a graduate student at Arizona State University, I found a poster, which I bought and hung on my wall. I've hung it in every apartment I've lived in since then and have it in my office today. It says, "You have two choices in life: you can dissolve into the mainstream, or you can be distinct. To be distinct, you must be different. To be different, you must strive to be what no one else but you can be . . ." I knew I was different, and the saying inspired me. It said I could go where others couldn't go *because* of my difference. Just last year I discovered that the author of the saying, Alan Ashley-Pitt, wasn't a philosopher or scientist. He wasn't even a real person. "Alan Ashley-Pitt" was a fictitious name made up by the poster company to sell posters. At first I was a little disappointed, but then I realized that a real person wrote it, only he or she didn't get credit, just like so many inventors whose contributions were overshadowed, forgotten, or erased.

▷ ▷ ▷

Much of my curiosity about flight came from the Wright brothers, who were also in my book of inventors. They are often credited for inventing the first airplane, but that's not entirely accurate. Like most of the inventions we've talked about, there were a lot of previous discoveries that aided the Wright brothers. The first attempts to get into the sky were in hot air balloons. According to author Jeffrey L. Ethell, in his book *Frontiers of Flight*, the first successful hot air balloon was launched by two French brothers, Joseph-Michel and Jacques-Étienne Montgolfier in September 1783. In order to see if the trip was survivable, their first passengers were non-human: a sheep, a duck, and a rooster. Fortunately, they survived. A successful human trip was achieved a month later. In 1900, the first hydrogen-filled, steerable dirigible made a successful flight, piloted by German Count Ferdinand von Zeppelin, which is how these dirigibles came to be called "zeppelins" (and also where the 1970s band Led Zeppelin got its name).

IT'S A BIRD, IT'S A PLANE

In the early 1800s, Sir George Cayley of Britain fulfilled a lifelong fascination with flying when he developed what would

Source: Wikimedia Commons

Sir George Cayley

become the key features of flight. Probably the most radical innovation was stabilizing the wings instead of having them flap like birds' wings. His glider looked a lot like the gliders of today. And he wrote a book, *On Aerial Navigation*, which described the three key elements to flight: lift, propulsion, and control. Lift is achieved by the shape of the wing. Propulsion is generated by the propeller or jet engine. Control comes from the vertical rudder on the tail and your steering.

The Wright brothers were helped by Cayley's ideas. From a young age, Orville and Wilbur were both interested in machinery and how things work. Orville never graduated high

Orville Wright   *Wilbur Wright*

school, but he loved taking things apart and studying them. Before they became interested in flight, the Wright brothers had a printing equipment business and then went on to build bicycles. Their ability to build things had a lot to do with their later success as aviators. They also had tremendous patience and discipline and used the "bottom-up" method to acquire as much knowledge as possible. In Fred Howard's biography of the brothers, he cites a letter they sent to the Smithsonian requesting information: "I am about to begin a systematic study of the subject . . . I wish to obtain such papers as the Smithsonian has published on this subject, and if possible a list

of other works in print in the English language." They went
on to build a series of planes to test their ideas, beginning with
gliders, then trying out lightweight gasoline engines and propellers. In 1902, according to Jeffrey L. Ethell in *Frontiers of
Flight,* they made between 700 and 1,000 successful glides in

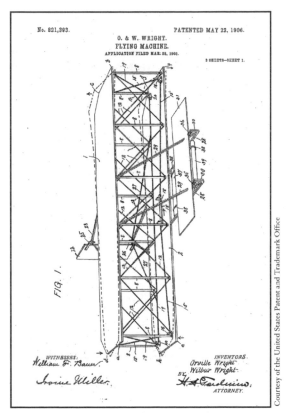

Patent No. US821393A for a flying machine by
Orville and Wilbur Wright

Kitty Hawk, North Carolina, testing and modifying with
each flight. According to Ethell, "For the first time in history,
a flying machine could be controlled through all three axes of
motion: pitch, yaw, and roll. The Wrights became the first

aviators to make stable turns. By the close of the season, they knew they had the basis for practical, powered flight." (Pitch is when the nose of the plane moves up and down. Roll is when the wings move left to right. And yaw is when the plane moves like the second hand of a clock to the right or left.) They received their first patent in 1903, for the "Flying Machine."

If the Wright brothers were around today, I think they might be diagnosed as somewhere on the autism or Asperger's spectrum. A lot of inventors would be, as they are people who typically spend hours and hours poring over the smallest detail and tirelessly focusing on a single project. Autism expert Simon Baron-Cohen of Cambridge University and mathematician Joan James of Oxford University have been studying the syndrome especially as it relates to the kind of special skills we've been talking about: musical abilities, computer skills, mathematics, engineering, etc. They are trying to determine whether geniuses Albert Einstein and Isaac Newton were on the Asperger's spectrum. While they acknowledge that it's ultimately impossible to diagnose a person after they are gone, both men showed signs of three key traits: obsessive interests, awkward social skills, and communication problems. Some of the Silicon Valley geniuses are thought to be on the spectrum. I found it interesting that a short article in the January 24, 1994, issue of *Time* magazine compared two *New Yorker* articles: an Oliver Sacks piece about me, and John Seabrook's article about Bill Gates. The article concluded that "in some ways, the articles were strongly and intriguingly similar." I think the main ways we might be similar are in terms of intensity, drive and focus about work, and perhaps a preference for work over socializing.

In my experience, people with autism who are able to get out and experience the world will continue to learn and lose or diminish some of their autistic traits as they age. Seabrook observed Gates rocking at meetings. I went back and watched the old videotapes of the Bill Gates antitrust depositions in 1998. His responses were awkward, and he either rocked or became silent when confronted with evidence; nowadays he looks relaxed and makes eye contact when he is interviewed or does public speaking. Over the years, I have become more comfortable socially as well. I attribute it to bottom-up thinking. In science, there are two models of learning: bottom up and top down. Top down is when you have a hypothesis and set about finding the data to prove it. Bottom up is when you gather data and arrive at the hypothesis. I am a bottom-up thinker and I've learned this way my whole life.

▷ ▷ ▷

Even after the disastrous results trying to fly my Guillow's glider, I was still excited (and a little anxious) about seeing whether I could re-create my childhood experiments with helicopters. I can't remember where I first got the idea to convert my glider into a helicopter, especially since it meant taking apart the plane, but my helicopter flew straight up in the air the first try. Only now, as an adult, my attempt to re-create liftoff didn't go so smoothly. I was in my kitchen, and I was actually a little worried about the helicopter hitting the kitchen ceiling; that's how sure I was it would launch. I twisted the rubber band until it was taut and let go. It turns out I didn't have to worry about the ceiling AT ALL because it immediately crashed to the floor. When I was a child, I observed that the helicopter's body spun almost as fast as the propeller, which prevented it from flying. I taped an index card to the body to stop it from spinning. My assumption was that the air resistance provided by the index card would solve it. I made a second attempt, winding the rubber band tighter, looked back up at the ceiling, hoping it wouldn't crash, and let her rip. Again, total flameout. The plane I had purchased at the hobby store had a smaller propeller, which had less lift.

This is always the moment when my inventor genes really kick in. There was no way I was going to accept defeat. I *had* to figure out how to make it fly. I decided the helicopter needed to be lighter, which led me to wonder if the tail was adding too much weight. It was then I took out my surgical tool (a kitchen knife) and performed the delicate surgery known as a "buttectomy," meaning I chopped off the tail.

I took my new and improved helicopter outside and decided to launch it from the ground. This time, it got about two inches off before nose-diving. I realized that the index card was too heavy, so I went back inside and replaced it with the original wings, shortening them to about half their original length. Now, the challenge was on. It was freezing outside, but I was determined to make my helicopter fly. I had figured this out as a kid; I wasn't about to give up as an adult with a PhD! Then it occurred to me that I needed to fly the helicopter into the wind to give it natural advantage, just as Homan Walsh flew his kite on the Canadian side of Niagara Falls to get the benefit of the westerly wind. On the fifth or sixth try it went a little higher, but it was hardly a success.

Back inside, I looked at the directions on the plastic sleeve again for any hint. It said to wind the rubber band clockwise and not to overwind it. I had noticed that the rubber band wasn't completely unwound after my failed efforts had landed. From this I deduced that the helicopter was underpowered. It needed more rpm, revolutions per minute. That was my aha! moment. I realized that I had to overcompensate for the weak propeller. To give it more power, I decided to overwind the rubber band, and I wound it like mad. I risked breaking it, but I had to get more rpm. I wasn't prepared to fail the FAA airworthiness test.

I took the little toy back out to the field. It was clouding over, and there was no one around; the only sound was a dog howling from somewhere inside a house. I was determined to figure out how to make the underpowered helicopter fly. This time, I decided to launch it from my hand, and it happened! The little helicopter flew for about eight seconds and got as high as eight or nine feet. Even after fifty years of engineering and developing systems, my heart did a somersault to see that little thing fly. In truth, it's no different from when I'm designing a piece of farm equipment. It's a lot of trial and error, it's running through variables and learning from each experiment. With my helicopter, I had to try different weights of paper for the wings, remove the tail, try different launch sites, fix rubber band slippage, gauge the wind direction, and finally overwind the rubber band. It was amazing how many variables there are in flying a balsa helicopter. Little details of design matter. And they matter a lot.

Courtesy of the author

This is the toy helicopter that I built.

In my cattle work, I was recently at a place where the animals refused to enter a chute. The plant manager had no idea why they wouldn't go. I saw it right away: a piece of paper towel had gotten caught on the chute and was waving like a flag. When I removed the towel, they moved. It was "hiding in plain sight." As a visual thinker, visual details are often obvious to me. I think this is also true for designers, architects, artists, mathematicians, and other thinkers who begin with an image.

◁ ◁ ◁ **SIMPLE HELICOPTER** ▷ ▷ ▷

You'll need:

- 1 plastic propeller with a plastic mount
- 1 Popsicle stick
- 1 paper clip
- Strapping tape, cut in thin pieces
- Index card
- Rubber bands
- Scissors

To create:

1. Place the plastic mounted propeller at one end of the Popsicle stick. Make certain the hold is firm.

2. Hold the paper clip so that you're looking at it head-on, and pull the inside part of the clip toward yourself so that it's bent at almost a 90-degree angle. Slide the end of the Popsicle stick that doesn't have the propeller on it between the two sides of the paper clip, and then use the strapping tape to tape the larger side firmly to the stick. This step is

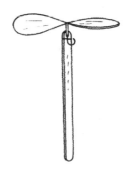

important as you don't want the paper clip flying off!

3. Take the index card and place it on a flat surface. (If you'd like, you can create and cut different designs on your index card, including butterflies, an actual helicopter shape, or a bird. The shape of the index card will not affect how the helicopter will fly, so have fun with this!) Tape the index card to the middle of the Popsicle stick.

4. Stretch one of the rubber bands with both hands and secure it on the hook that is part of the propeller mount and through the part of the paper clip that's sticking out.

5. Spin the propeller to wind the rubber band enough times so that it is completely coiled and then some.

6. To fly your helicopter, hold the top of the propeller and the lower end of the Popsicle stick near the paper clip. Let go of the top first and, a second later, let go of the bottom.

7. Experiment with different thicknesses and lengths of rubber bands for different types of energy for your helicopter. Also, experiment with different propellers and with only using part of an index card.

THE FORGOTTEN ALPHONSE PÉNAUD

It was a little toy helicopter made of cork, bamboo, and paper given to them by their father that first got the Wright brothers interested in flight. The inventor of the helicopter was a Frenchman named Alphonse Pénaud who was the first

Alphonse Pénaud

inventor we know of to figure out how to power a toy airplane with rubber bands, twisting them from the propeller to the tail to power up the propeller. He went on to build something called the "planophore," which added two crucial elements. He

curved the wings upward, which we talked about, and he added a rear-mounted stabilizer. The HBO movie about my life shows how I made a helicopter out of a toy airplane. Only

they had to use camera tricks to make it fly. It was too heavy to fly straight up because they left the wheel assembly on it. The wheel assembly has to be removed. Details!

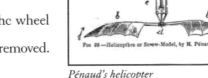

Pénaud's helicopter

Even more than the helicopters I used to experiment with, I wanted to see if I could re-create my childhood parachute. This was another passion of mine. I loved watching parachutes sail through the sky, especially the moment when the parachute opens, catches the air, and gently floats to earth. Toy parachutes were fairly common in the fifties. We had all seen the brave men of World War II parachuting out of planes. I had a plastic one that was folded inside a straw. You launched it by blowing into the straw like a blowgun. Like most things I encountered that involved flight, I set out to make my own, which usually began by raiding our fabric bag and seizing my mother's cast-off silk scarves.

When I set out to re-create the project, I remembered two crucial things from my childhood project. First I had to make a crossbar to keep the strings from twisting up. Then I had to give the parachute sufficient weight in order to stabilize it. I no longer remember how many months it took me to figure out these key components when I was kid, but once again I thought it would be pretty easy to duplicate as an adult. Ha!

I needed to punch holes through the four corners of the scarf for the strings. I improvised with a pointed can opener because I was afraid that using scissors would tear too much of the fabric. Then I used pliers to cut two lengths of wire from a hanger. Next, I curled up each end of the wires, also with the pliers, to make four loops. I crossed the two wires and used duct tape to hold them together. Then I attached the strings from each corner of the scarf to the wire loops. Last, I hung a metal pen from the center of the crossbars to serve as the paratrooper. A plastic toy soldier would have been too light.

Off I went back to the field. It was time to start using trial and error again at Area 51, conducting my top-secret military aeronau-

Courtesy of the author

Here is the parachute that I built

tical experiments. I swung the blue parachute into the air. First launch: fail. I noticed right away that the pen was tilted, which threw off stability; plus it didn't seem heavy enough. That was just my instinct so I straightened the pen and taped a few pennies on to give it more weight. It still failed to open on my next launch, but at least the strings weren't tangling. Then I wondered about how I was launching it: into the wind or away from it. I tried both. Both failed. Epic fail. It was freezing outside by then, the sun was going down, and I made a quick decision to shorten the strings right on the spot. I tied loops in case I was incorrect and they'd need to be lengthened. Once again, I swung the parachute over my head and into the air. When it reached about twelve feet, the scarf opened, and it came drifting down to earth. Even though I'm almost seventy years old,

I felt like I was seven. It is the thrill of making it work and watching the graceful beauty of a parachute sailing to earth on nothing but air.

◁ ◁ ◁ **PARACHUTE** ▷ ▷ ▷

You'll need:

- Scissors
- 1 20-inch-x-20-inch (approximately) piece of light plastic or cloth, or a lightweight scarf
- Duct tape
- 4 15-inch-long pieces of string (experiment with different lengths)
- 1 6-inch-long piece of string
- Pliers
- Wire coat hanger
- A Matchbox car, small toy, and assorted coins, so you can experiment with different amounts of weight

To create:

1. If it's not already the right size, use your scissors to cut the cloth, plastic, or scarf into a square approximately 20 inches long and wide. Cut a

small hole at each corner. If you're using plastic, use tape to reinforce the holes to prevent tearing.

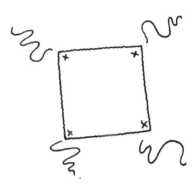

2. Tie one end of each of the four 15-inch-long pieces of string through the holes at each corner.

3. To make a "spreader," which will keep your strings from tangling, use pliers to cut two equal lengths (about 6 inches long) of hanger wire. You will probably have to work the pliers back and forth against the wire to cut it into pieces. Cross the pieces of hanger wire and secure them into the cross shape with duct tape. Curl the end of each wire up into a loop. The finished cross will be approximately 4 inches wide after the ends are bent into loops.

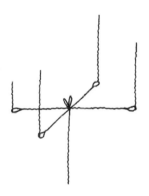

4. Tie the other ends of the four strings to the loops of the spreader. (In the photo of my parachute, you can see some loops in the strings. The loops enabled me to experiment with string length without cutting the strings.)

5. Now use your small toy and some coins for extra weight, and attach them with the shorter piece of string to the center of the spreader—letting the weighted object hang down a few inches. You must experiment so that the spread assembly remains level when the coins and/or toy are suspended from it.

6. To launch the parachute, fold the parachute material in half and half again. Bring the weight up to the parachute. Toss in the air or drop from a window. The parachute will open as it falls. Another way to launch it is to hold the top of the canopy and sling it into the air.

Experimenting is about variables, creative thinking, and patience. In my engineering work, I call it "project loyalty," which means I am dedicated to making things work. In 1976, researchers at the University of Connecticut were developing a conveyor restrainer for holding animals. They had a laboratory prototype to demonstrate how their method of holding animals was low stress, only they had no idea if it would actually work. The Humane Society contacted me because of a paper I had written about humane cattle handling.

The first thing I noticed was that the engineers had not

developed a method to make the restrainer fit different-size animals. I experimented with plywood to make a device that would prevent the animals from toppling sideways on the conveyor by narrowing the top portion of the outer frame. However, if the bottom part was too narrow, the animals would not be able to straddle the conveyor, and their hips and shoulders would get pinched. That's when I realized the side panels needed to move in and out on a parallelogram hinge. A parallelogram hinge enables the side panels to remain vertical when the space between them is widened or narrowed. Since it is a parallelogram, the sides will also move up and down as they move in and out. But the key involved something radical. I saw that turning the apparatus upside down better accommodated the animal's shape because the space for the animal's hip joint would widen at the same time as the body space widened. I knew all this because of my experience handling cattle and making equipment. As the expression goes, you have to get your hands dirty.

Not too long ago, I visited Pixar Animation Studios, the company responsible for movies such as *Toy Story*, *Cars*, and *Finding Nemo*. I witnessed something incredible. I've seen some good drawings created on computer, but the people who draw best on computers know how to draw by hand first. They told me at Pixar that sometimes they have to get their artists *off* their computers and drawing by hand to bring the character to life. I have observed the same in my own industry: The best designers have learned to draw by hand or have actually built things. The worst drawings come from people who have never used their hands. They do not "see" what they have drawn. Recently I received a drawing where the cattle would actually have to walk through a concrete wall to go through a chute. It was obvious that the person who had drawn this on the computer was not seeing it.

At another animation company I saw a huge 3-D printer that produced statues of cartoon characters about six inches tall. The artists kept the models next to their mouse pads within reach because you have to touch to perceive. The mouse is not hooked up to the brain in the same way. The best work comes from the artist who understands the feel of things in addition to the technology. You have to touch to perceive; it's that simple. You have to touch to perceive.

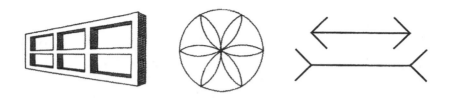

· CHAPTER FIVE ·

OPTICAL ILLUSIONS

Our mother allowed me and my siblings to watch television for exactly one hour a day, and we had to watch pre-approved shows. If we misbehaved, it was the first thing she took away, and then our allowance. I really wanted to watch my TV programs, so I behaved most of the time. One of my favorites was a science fiction program called *The Outer Limits*. It always started with voiceover: *There is nothing wrong with your television set. Do not attempt to adjust the picture . . . We repeat there is nothing wrong with your television set. You are about to participate in a great adventure. You are about to experience the awe and mystery which reaches from the inner mind to—The Outer Limits.* The most famous episode was about the Earth being invaded by insect-like aliens from another planet. I loved stuff like that.

I was also the kind of kid who could just as easily spend hours by myself in my bedroom at my worktable. I'd have been a prime candidate for video game addiction if the games had been around. My worktable had once been our kitchen table. Unlike a desk with books and papers, it was my personal laboratory, and it's where I could noodle around taking things apart and putting them back together.

My next-door neighbors had a fantastic Erector Set that we used to make robots and buildings. The Erector Set came with its own set of tools to fasten all the little bolts and nuts, which was right up my alley. But I didn't stop there. I would turn old electric clock motors or broken appliances into robots using my father's extensive tool collection. Every bit of wire, every screw and plug was treasure to me.

HELLO BOYS! MAKE LOTS OF TOYS!*

A. C. Gilbert, the inventor of Erector Sets, worked as a magician to pay for his college education, and in his senior year he formed the Mysto Manufacturing Company, which sold magic sets. According to the website Girders & Gears, Gilbert came up with the idea of the Erector Set during his train rides from Yale, in New Haven, Connecticut, to New York City, when he witnessed the steel girders being installed for electrical power lines. Gilbert's genius was in creating a toy that didn't feel like a toy. The kit came with felt, beams, screws, nuts, bolts, gears, pulleys, and in later models actual motors. You could build bridges, skyscrapers, windmills . . .

Source: Wikimedia Commons

A. C. Gilbert

just about anything you could dream up. His kits became more elaborate; later ones included steam shovels, Ferris wheels, and even a zeppelin. One of his most prized kits came with blueprints for the "Mysterious Walking Giant" robot. The Erector Set was the first American toy to have a major ad campaign and quickly became one of the most popular toys of all time.

*Company slogan. Totally sexist!

By experimenting for hours with my projects, I learned the most essential tools the scientist needs: deductive reasoning (which is using logic to arrive at an answer after considering all the possibilities), problem solving, and patience. I also learned basic work skills as a kid. My siblings and I always had chores and part-time jobs growing up. There is no way you are going to get a job if you spend all your time playing video games. Even if you want your job to be designing video games! At the least you would need to learn coding, design, electronics, and storytelling. Today there is also a huge shortage of skilled workers. One of the worst things our schools have done is removing hands-on classes such as shop, welding, and auto mechanics. You need to develop the skills to make things. These skills were never tested more than when I set my sights on re-creating the Ames room.

When I was in high school, our teachers showed us a movie about optical illusions from Bell Labs. Alexander Graham Bell was one of my inventor heroes. I was always inspired by a famous quote of his, "When one door closes, another door opens, but we so often look so long and regretfully upon the closed door, that we do not see the ones which open for us." I understand that Bell was using the idea of a door as a metaphor, but ever since high school, and as a visual thinker, I held the picture of a physical door in my mind whenever I faced a new challenge. I used to go out onto the roof of my dormitory to look at the stars. One evening, I noticed a little door that led to another, larger section of the roof. I can still see that door in my mind, and other doors later in my life when I had to push myself through and face fear. Change is difficult for most people but especially people with autism; our nervous systems take longer to process new things.

▷ ▷ ▷

CAN YOU HEAR ME?
CAN YOU HEAR ME NOW?

....

It makes sense that Alexander Graham Bell turned his inventive mind toward communication. His grandfather, father, and brother were speech teachers, and Bell's mother

Source: Wikimedia Commons

Alexander Graham Bell

and wife were deaf. Bell worked as a professor of vocal physiology and mechanics of speech before starting his own school for the deaf. The Volta Laboratory was dedicated to finding the causes of deafness. Bell helped Helen Keller continue her education and remained a lifelong bene-

factor. She even dedicated her autobiography, *The Story of My Life*, to him with the words: "To Alexander Graham Bell, who has taught the deaf to speak and enabled the listening ear to hear speech from the Atlantic to the Rockies."

We mostly remember that Bell invented the telephone. The American Telephone and Telegraph Company (AT&T), founded in the 1870s, acquired several smaller companies, including the Western Electric Company, founded by Bell's rival, Elisha Gray, and became the largest communications and technology company in the country. Western manufactured the phone cases and switchboards. AT&T provided the technology. You can think of Western as providing the hardware and AT&T providing the software. Alexander Graham Bell also created Bell Labs, which fostered experimentation and innovation. Over time, they went on to develop many technologies, including one accidental discovery that changed the way we understand the galaxies. Physicist and engineer Karl Jansky was trying to figure out what was causing static on shortwave radios when he discovered radio astronomy, which uses radio telescopes to measure things like galaxies and quasars and provides evidence of the big bang theory.

Four decades later, Shirley Ann Jackson, a theoretical physicist and the first black woman to be awarded a PhD from MIT, made another astonishing breakthrough while working at Bell Labs. Her research on subatomic particles paved the way for fax machines, touch tone phones, solar cells, fiber-optic cables, and the technology behind caller ID and call waiting. Jackson's accomplishments can be traced back to her childhood when she graduated first

Shirley Ann Jackson

Source: World Economic Forum via Wikimedia Commons

in her high school class. What I think is so incredible about Shirley Jackson is that she went beyond the laboratory to share her knowledge and make a difference. She served as chairman of the U.S. Nuclear Regulatory Commission under President Bill Clinton, and today she is the first African American female president of Rensselaer Polytechnic University, which is the oldest technological research university in the U.S.

THE PATENT THAT WENT TO THE SUPREME COURT

Most people have never heard of Elisha Gray, but some people still think he deserved the U.S. patent for the telephone.

It was Valentine's Day, February 14, in 1876, when Gray filed a "caveat" with the patent office, which is an application not quite ready to be evaluated. It's kind of like a place-holder. Two hours later, Alexander Graham Bell filed his patent application. Some scholars think that

Elisha Gray

Source: Wikimed a Commons

Bell was privy to the caveat and stole Gray's ideas. Others argue that Bell had been working on the technology for years and the proof was in his notebooks. There are all kinds of stories of bribes and greedy lawyers, and after many court battles, the case went all the way to the Supreme Court of the United States, which upheld the Bell patents.

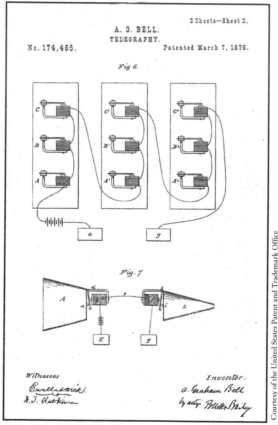

Patent No. US174465A for improvements in telegraphy by Alexander Graham Bell

▷ ▷ ▷

The Ames room looked really cool. I had already learned about the Müller-Lyer illusion in grade school and liked optical illusions because they play with the way we think we see things. The Müller-Lyer illusion looks incredibly simple, but scientists still disagree on what exactly is responsible for the illusion. Some think it's because of the way our brains process depth and distance; others think it has to with how our eyes move. The illusion consists of three lines of the same length, with arrows on each end. Two arrows face out, two face in, and the third has both arrows pointing to the left. With the arrows attached, the lines look like they are of different lengths. I used a ruler and drew a Müller-Lyer illusion. The line with the arrows pointed outward appeared longer. I measured the lines again to convince myself that I had not measured them incorrectly. They were both the same length. I deduced that the line looks longer when the arrows are pointed outward because the entire drawing is longer.

◁ ◁ ◁ MÜLLER-LYER ILLUSION ▷ ▷ ▷

You'll need:

- Ruler
- Pen
- Paper

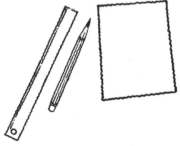

To create:

1. Using the ruler and pen, draw two parallel lines that are exactly the same length on your piece of paper.

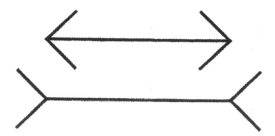

2. On one line, draw arrows that point inward. On the other line, draw arrows that point outward.

3. Ask your friends which line is longer. Have them measure the two lines and watch their surprised looks when they learn the lines are the exact same size!

In the movie we saw in high school, the Ames room showed a room with two men, one standing at either end. One man was twice as big as the other. Only when they step outside the room, you see that they are exactly the same size! I couldn't believe my eyes and couldn't stop thinking about it. I knew there was some kind of trick, but I couldn't figure it out. When I asked Mr. Burns, my psychology teacher, how it was done, he challenged me to make my own Ames room. I thought it would take a day or two. After all, I had already successfully made an Ames trapezoidal window, which is why I figured the illusion had something to do with depth perception. Only the Ames trapezoidal window is a one-dimensional illusion. The window looks like a normal rectangular window, but when you rotate it slowly, it looks as if the window is moving back and forth (oscillating), instead of going around (rotating). Your mind knows that's not possible, but changing the perspective changes the way the brain perceives. That's what Ames was all about.

◀ ◀ ◀ AMES TRAPEZOIDAL WINDOW ▷ ▷ ▷

You'll need:

- Cardboard
- Ruler
- Pencil
- Markers (including one black one) and/or acrylic paint
- Paintbrushes
- Scissors or X-Acto knife
- String
- Tape

To create:

1. Draw the image to the right (you can copy and enlarge it to any size you like) onto the cardboard using the ruler and pencil. Draw the same

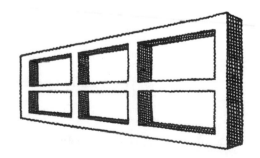

image on both sides of the cardboard. (When I first
built the Ames window, all I had was the Bell Labs
movie. I challenge you to take a brief look at the
image and then try to create it without tracing it.)

2. Use the markers and acrylic paint to color in the
    image. Outline the design with a black marker.

3. Cut out the interiors of the windows with scissors or
    an X-Acto knife.

4. Use string to suspend the
    cardboard vertically from an
    overhead object, such as a lamp,
    and set it spinning in circles.
    Spinning provides the illusion that
    the windows are rotating through
    less than 180 degrees. Instead,
    they will appear to be swinging
    back and forth at a regular speed
    like a pendulum. Try rotating the
    window at different speeds, and
    observe how the illusion may vary
    between rotation and moving back and forth.

5. For another special effect, place a pencil in the corner
    of the middle window and tape it in place. Spin the
    cardboard. The pencil appears to go through the
    window frame.

I started my Ames room by experimenting with the shape of the room. The one I had seen in the movie looked like a shoe box, so I started with a rectangular room. I guessed that there was either a fake ceiling or a tilted floor to explain the difference in the size of the men. I must have built ten different floors and ceilings, but nothing worked. Then I went back and looked at the original shape of the room. Maybe it was square. Then I imagined the illusion had something to do with the depth. I built my box so it was deeper than it was wide. It still didn't work, but I continued to try one small adjustment after another. I felt pretty defeated when I went back to my teacher one month later having made no progress. He took pity on me and gave me a two-second peek at a book that gave me a single but crucial hint.

The front of the room was in the shape of a trapezoid!

*People in an Ames illusion room in the Villette science
museum in France*

I wish I could say that it all clicked in my brain when my teacher gave me the hint, and that I figured it out on the spot, but it still took more trial and error on my part. When you look at an Ames room, you look with one eye through a pinhole. The reason for this is you need to block out the usual clues we get from depth perception for the illusion to work. That's why it's officially called the monocular Ames distorted room illusion.

This is the Ames illusion room that I created for this book

These are the two horses that I used in my Ames room— they are clearly the same size

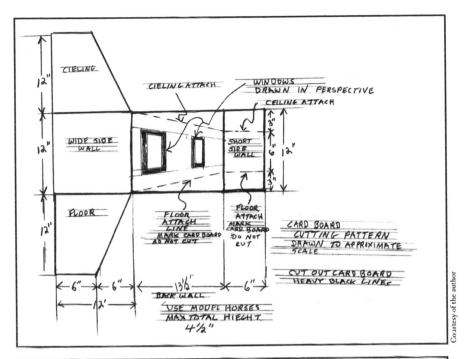

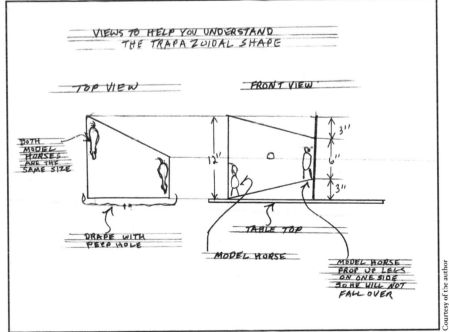

My schematics for an Ames illusion room

LOVE IS BLIND

....

Adelbert Ames Jr. was a scientist, ophthalmologist, and pioneer of physiological optics. After studying law at Harvard, Ames received a fellowship from Clark University to study physiological optics, which led to his discovery of anieseikonia, a condition where a person misperceives shapes, sizes, and the locations of objects. I think it's interesting

Source: Wikimedia Commons

Adelbert Ames Jr.

that most of Ames's experiments challenge the viewer's perceptions by distorting them. Ames invented instruments used to diagnose and test vision. Some will look pretty familiar from your eye doctor's office. Roy R. Behrens, Professor of Art at the University of Northern Iowa, concludes that much of Ames's work has more appeal for the artist than for the scientist. As a visual thinker, I have to disagree. Ames wanted to see if he could change the way we perceive. He definitely changed the way I look at things and taught me to look more closely because things are not always as they appear. In fact, much of my success in working with animals is due to my ability to perceive what others do not. It may explain part of why I was so obsessed with Ames in high school.

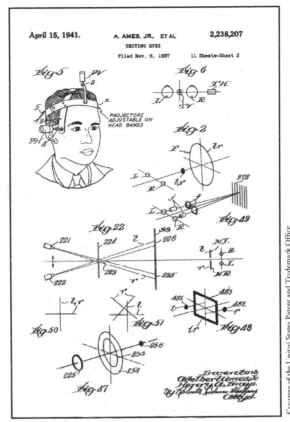

Patent No. US2238207A for testing eyes by Adelbert Ames Jr.

Have you ever heard of a laserphaco probe? No, it's not from the starship *Enterprise*. It's a medical instrument that uses a laser to remove cataracts from the eyes. Cataracts are formed when the lens of the eye gets blurry, usually because of ageing or injury. In 1988, Patricia Bath was the first female African American doctor to receive a medical patent. Her probe has the ability to prevent blindness due to cataracts and is used all around the world. In high school, Bath was inspired by the work of humanitarian Albert Schweitzer, who aided people with leprosy in the Congo. She would later devote her-self to something called "community ophthalmology," whose mission is to offer vision care to all people. Bath then co-founded the American Institute for the Prevention of Blindness. Like mem-bers of Doctors Without Borders, she has traveled the world: her mission is to ensure good eye care and the prevention of blindness. "The ability to restore sight," she says, "is the ultimate reward."

Patricia Bath

Source: Wikimedia Commons

When I was a teenager, I was also fascinated by the stereoscope invented by Charles Wheatstone in 1838. With its illusion of 3-D, it was one of the most popular scientific toys of its day. Unlike the Ames room, which depends on monocular vision, the stereoscope takes advantage of binocular vision. Each one of your eyes sees the world from a slightly different angle, and your brain puts them together into one image that also has depth perception. This is called binocular vision. It's the same principle used in 3-D movies. The 3-D glasses have one red and one blue lens. The screen dis-plays two images, and the glasses work as a filter so each eye only sees one image, and your brain puts them together such that they appear three-dimensional. To create a picture for a stereoscope, two photos are taken with two cameras that are beside each other. The distance between the two camera lenses is approximately 2.6 inches, which is the same spacing as the distance between a person's eyes. When you look at the photos through the two lenses of a stereoscope, the image appears in 3-D. You can make your own stereoscope. I bought one when I was in college at an antique store in Fitzwilliam, New Hampshire, along with a bunch of stereo cards of people diving off a pier, kids setting off firecrackers, and Niagara Falls.

An example of antique stereotype images

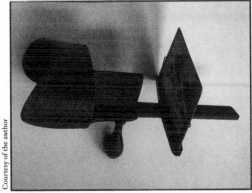

This is an antique stereoscope that I had purchased

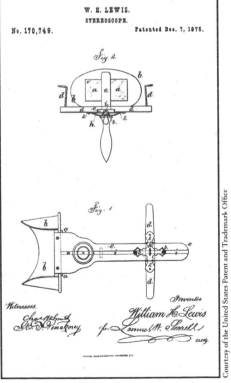

Patent No. US170749A for improvement in stereoscopes by William H. Lewis

◀ ◀ ◀ **STEREOSCOPE** ▷ ▷ ▷

You'll need:

- Cheap reading glasses with a magnifying power of 3.0 (found at most drugstores)

- 4-x-8-inch piece of cardboard

- Pencil

- Scissors

- E6000 glue

- 2 old yardsticks you can cut up

- Small saw

- Wood glue

- Hammer

- Finishing nails

- ½-x-5-inch strip of flexible crafting metal or super duty steel strapping coil

- Epoxy or Super Glue for gluing metal strip

- Small binder clip

- 2-x-4-inch piece of cardboard

- 2-inch alligator clip

- Stereoview photographs (You can often find these in flea markets or antique stores, or you can make your own by taking and printing pictures from your camera that are nearly identical. You can use two cameras spaced 2.6 inches apart, which is equal to the width between your eyes. For still scenes, a single camera is moved after the first picture is taken. It may work best if the people or objects are about 6 feet away.)

To create:

1. Pop the lenses out of the reading glasses frames.

2. Place the lenses on the 4-x-8-inch piece of cardboard at the same distance apart as they were when they were in the frames. Trace their shape on the cardboard.

3. Use scissors to cut out holes just inside your tracing lines so the holes are slightly smaller than the lenses. The left hole will line up with the center of the left photograph of your stereoview picture, and the right hole will line up with the center of the right photograph. Using the E6000 glue, carefully glue around the back edge of the lenses and stick them to the two holes in the front of the cardboard. (Before gluing, experiment with the angle of the lenses, tilting one side of them slightly forward.) Let dry several hours.

4. Cut up the yardsticks using a small saw. Cut the first one into three pieces: a 4-inch-long piece, a 15-inch-long piece, and a 9-inch-long piece. Cut the second yardstick into a 15-inch-long piece. Discard the remaining parts of both yardsticks.

5. Now, create your stereoview base. With wood glue, a hammer, and finishing nails, attach the 4-inch piece of yardstick vertically on the end of a 15-inch piece of yardstick.

GLUE

6. Create a "belt" or "slide" out of the flexible metal. Place the second 15-inch piece of wood flat atop the 15-inch part of the base you just created and wrap the metal around a single time until the ends cross each other, and make sure that it's loose enough so that you can feel that the top base piece will slide when pulled. Keeping track of where the two ends met, remove the slide from the base and use the epoxy or Super Glue to seal the overlapping ends of the metal together. Clip

with the binder clip to create a firm hold while the glue dries. Remove binder clip after the glue has dried. When the two ends are firmly glued, slip this "belt" or "slide" back onto the two base pieces of yardstick. It will move around freely but will allow you to slide a photo back and forth.

7. Use E6000 glue to attach the piece of cardboard with the lenses on it an inch from the top of the 4-inch lens-holder piece of yardstick so that it's sticking up above the end of the yardstick piece and the lenses are positioned so that they are looking out over the 15-inch base piece. Allow to dry several hours.

8. To keep the views from the two eyes separated, mount a piece of cardboard perpendicularly between the two lenses. (See the photo of my antique stereoscope on page 189 for reference.)

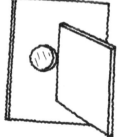

9. Use wood glue and the hammer and finishing nails to attach the 9-inch photo-holder piece of wood to the end of the upper 15-inch piece of yardstick (opposite the 4-inch piece). Allow to dry. Attach the alligator clip about ½ an inch below the top of the 9-inch piece of yardstick on the side facing the lenses. Glue with E6000 and allow to dry for several hours. The alligator clip will hold your photo.

10. Look through the lenses and hold the stereoview
    photograph up at the distance that works best for
    you. Move the top base back and forth until you get
    a 3-D effect. When the effect of the cardboard works
    correctly and forces each of your eyes to see each
    image separately, the two pictures will merge into one.

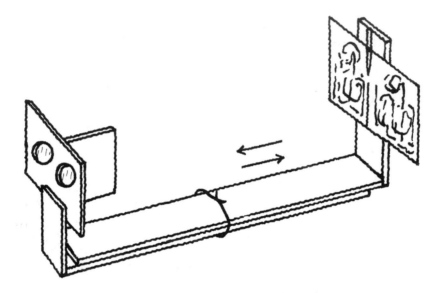

THE THIRD DIMENSION

You've probably heard of Oculus Rift. It's the 3-D headset for
reality games. It's pretty cool, but it owes a lot to the humble
stereoscope because the same principles are at work. In fact, if
you look up the patents for Oculus Rift, the claim is for "the
ornamental design of a virtual reality headset." The creator,

Palmer Luckey, was able to patent only the outer gear because you can't patent the way two eyes look at something. The thing that most impresses me about Palmer Luckey was that he was a die-hard tinkerer who was building things in his family's garage since he was a kid. According to *Vanity Fair* journalist Max Chafkin, he built his own computers and paid for his hobbies by buying broken iPhones on eBay, then fixing and reselling them.

In 2009, when he was seventeen, Luckey started building the prototype for Oculus Rift in his parents' garage. At nineteen, he ran a Kickstarter campaign to get his headset project off the ground. He raised $2.4 million and eventually sold his invention to Facebook founder Mark Zuckerberg for $2 billion. I tried the headset out at a Facebook display at the Denver airport. It showed a scene of animals approaching people and traveling by boat. It looked a lot like 3-D movies. The main difference was that I could turn my head and see a side view of the scene, which was cool.

Eventually, I did figure out how to make the Ames room, and the secret has a lot in common with Oculus Rift: it was a three-dimensional trapezoid. The floor, ceiling, and walls were ALL trapezoids. I had not been able to tell that from the photo. I'm still not sure how the eureka! moment happened; maybe it was because

I couldn't think about anything else for over a month. Though sometimes they say the best way to figure something out is to *stop* thinking about it. But I finally had a flash of insight to build it as a three-dimensional trapezoid. Once I figured it out, I couldn't build it fast enough.

One of the most beneficial aspects of making the Ames room in high school was that I proved to myself that I could finish something no matter how difficult it seemed. My teacher did the right thing by making me figure it out on my own. I was incredibly proud when my project was selected to be exhibited when the board of trustees of the school came to visit. I really felt important. I still think about Ames's ideas about perception when I'm working with animals and trying to translate what they see, like shadows, heights, or the surfaces of different floorings, and how it impacts their movement. If I can envision the environment from the point of view of the animal, I can figure out how the animal will behave. It's all about perception.

When I decided to see if I could create the room as an adult, it turned out to be pretty easy because I never forgot that one vital piece of information about trapezoids. Re-creating it was actually a lot of fun. I bought stiff cardboard, tape, and two model horses the exact same size and shape. You can use any two figures you like, as long as they are the same size. I hunted around and found my grandfather's drafting tools. I was very proud when he gave them to me before he died. All you need for the Ames room is a ruler, a protractor for measuring angles, and heavy-duty scissors or an X-Acto knife. To further enhance the illusion, you can add windows drawn in the shape of vertical trapezoids. It is the same as drawing windows in perspective. The checkerboard floor is drawn in perspective as well with bigger squares on the floor located at the large end of the trapezoid. The squares get progressively smaller toward the small end of the trapezoid. You can experiment with all sorts of decorations (visual information) to increase the illusion.

◁ ◁ ◁ AMES ILLUSION ROOM ▷ ▷ ▷

You'll need:

- Pencil
- 1 piece of paper for the miniature Ames room that you can create using these instructions (Use cardboard and a ruler if you'd like to follow the larger plan on page 185.)
- Scissors
- Markers
- Tape
- 2 equal-size figurines
- Small piece of cloth

To create:

1. Trace the image on the next page onto your piece of paper and use your scissors to cut it

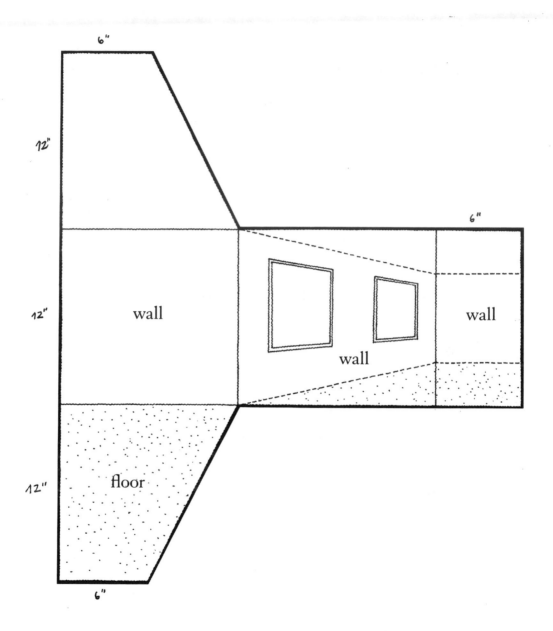

out along the thicker solid lines.

2. Use your markers to decorate the floor in the area labeled "floor" and decorate the walls in the areas

labeled "wall" (I made two
windows on the wall that
was angled, like in the
drawing).

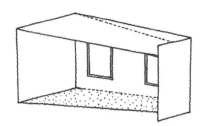

3. Fold the diagram on the
    thinner solid lines.

4. Start taping the edges together. For the short-side-
    wall section, tape along the dotted line instead of the
    solid line to attach the ceiling and the floor.

5. When you have taped it all together, you should have
    one open side, which will
    be the front of your room.
    Put your room on a flat
    surface floor-side down
    and add the 2 figurines (I
    used horses).

6. Cut your piece of cloth
    so that it is big enough to
    fully cover the one open
    side. Cut a small hole in
    the middle of the cloth,
    and then tape the cloth
    along the top of the room
    so that it hangs down as
    the final wall.

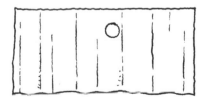

7. Look through the hole in your cloth.
   You will notice that the toys appear to be
   different sizes!

I also loved making dioramas. I first saw professional dioramas at the American Museum of Natural History in New York City. Dioramas (a word that comes from the Greek "to see through") became a popular feature of natural history museums, many of which were built in the late nineteenth and early twentieth centuries. The aim was to give people the most scientifically accurate portrait of natural habitats and animal life. Diorama artists strive to make animals and their habitats as authentic as possible. The animals themselves are made from real animal skins that are stitched around forms. I often had the feeling that the animals might bust out of their glass exhibits and come to life like in the movie *Night at the Museum*.

Even though I was always most interested in the animals, I also wondered who the artists were who created the dioramas. As a visual thinker, I was curious about how they painted the curved walls and domed ceilings, and made them look realistic.

◁ ◁ ◁ SOLAR SYSTEM DIORAMA ▷ ▷ ▷

You'll need:

- Large shoe box

- Acrylic paints (black, silver, gold, and any other colors you like)
- Paintbrushes
- White paint pen
- Assorted sizes of polystyrene or Styrofoam balls

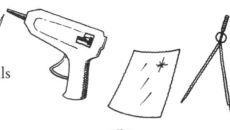

- Bamboo skewers
- Large drinking glasses
- Compass
- Gold paper
- Scissors
- Tombow glue, or any other multipurpose glue that is repositionable with a permanent bond
- Large needle
- Clear beading thread
- Scotch tape
- Black construction paper
- Pin
- Flashlight

To create:

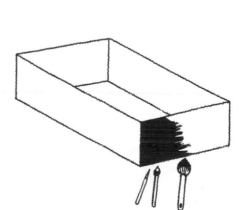

1. Paint the inside and the outside of the box with black paint and allow to dry thoroughly,

preferably overnight.

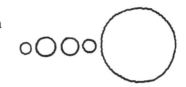

2. Add different-size white dots with the white paint pen to represent the stars.

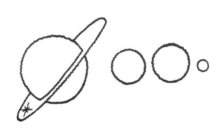

3. Check online or in a solar system book for the sizes and colors of the planets. Place the "planets" (the polystyrene or Styrofoam balls) on skewers and paint them their appropriate colors. Stand each in a large glass to dry. To create Saturn's rings, use a compass and draw two concentric circles on the gold paper, the smaller of which should be the circumference of the polystyrene of Styrofoam ball you are using. Using your scissors, cut out and affix with glue around the middle of Saturn.

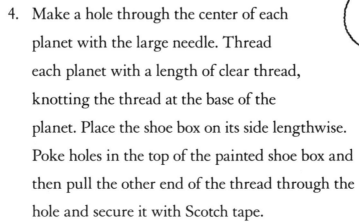

4. Make a hole through the center of each planet with the large needle. Thread each planet with a length of clear thread, knotting the thread at the base of the planet. Place the shoe box on its side lengthwise. Poke holes in the top of the painted shoe box and then pull the other end of the thread through the hole and secure it with Scotch tape.

5. Cover the side of your shoe box with black paper to hide the threads.

6. Poke holes with a pin in the back of the box. Shine a flashlight behind the holes and watch your galaxy glow.

In a book of essays called *Natural History Dioramas*, contributor Michael Anderson identifies one painter in particular who, in the 1930s, applied scientific principles to the problem of perspective in painting the dome-shaped walls. Trained as an architect, James Perry Wilson projected grids onto the diorama walls. This allowed far more accuracy than painting freehand. His method is similar to "projective geometry," which is a branch of mathematics that measures the effect of projecting images. Two very basic examples of projective geometry are shadows cast on a wall or movies projected on a screen. You can easily test this by shining a flashlight on the wall. If you shine it at a 90-degree angle, the circumference of the protective glass and the circle on the wall will be proportionately the same. What gets really interesting is when you shine the light at

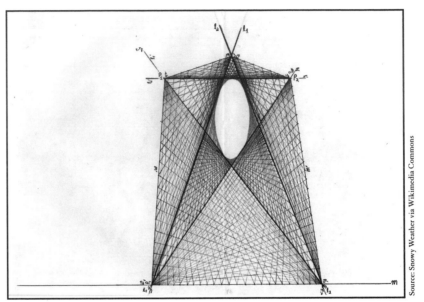

An example of projective geometry

different angles. Check out Google Images for "projective geometry." The graphics are fantastic.

For my own smaller dioramas, I'd glue magazine pictures on the inside of a box from the grocery store, transforming it into a ranch. Back when I was a kid, cigarette companies could still advertise in magazines, and the Marlboro ads had the best backgrounds of the west. I'd add small plants for the trees, and sticks became fences where you could tie up your horse. I made a trough out of bark. Our cat used to shed a lot, and I'd ball up the hair and make tumbleweed. I'd glue plain old dirt from our backyard for the ground. Last, I'd take a few of the figurines from my plastic set and glue them to the floor as well. To make the scene look three-dimensional, I'd place some figures close to the front of the box and others toward the back of the box. Then I'd cover the box with a sheet, cut a hole in it, as you do with the Ames room, and peer inside. Looking at the diorama with monocular vision made it appear three-dimensional.

I also made dioramas of people in the jungle among a thicket of leafy branches. I made street scenes with lampposts and fire hydrants. The fun was coming up with the way to get the details right. Each diorama provided different opportunities to play with depth perception and 3-D vision. I wish I had kept them.

▷ ▷ ▷

Drafting is the key to building almost anything. The first step is to learn to read blueprints and engineering drawings. My first exposure to drafting was in art class, where we drew flower patterns with a compass. It's super-easy. All you need is a compass, a pencil, and paper.

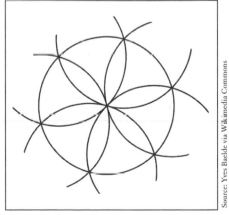

A compass flower

Source: Yves Baelde via Wikimedia Commons

◄ ◄ ◄ COMPASS FLOWER ▷ ▷ ▷

You'll need:

- 1 sheet of paper
- Compass
- Crayons, markers, or colored pencils

To create:

1. Draw a circle, any size, in the center of your piece of paper.

2. Place the point of your compass on any point of the circle, and draw a semicircle inside the circle.

3. Take the point of your compass and place it where the previous line intersects on the circle and draw another semicircle.

4. Keep moving the compass counterclockwise, placing its point at the next intersect. With a few strokes of your compass, you will have six symmetrical points of a flower.

5. Embellish your flower with crayons, markers, or colored pencils.

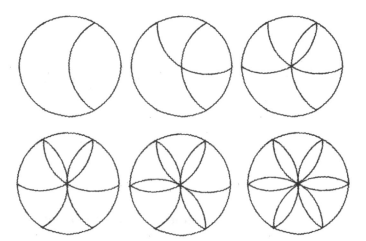

I've seen a lot of errors on designs occur because you can't feel where the center of the circle is on a computer. Drawing circles

Me drawing a compass flower

with a compass allows you to experience circles both with your eyes and with your hands. To draw a perfect circle, all you need is a compass. You can make a simple flower or an incredibly complex design.

The next step in drafting and understanding blueprints is being able to relate the lines on the drawing to the real structure. I didn't use any plans for my first two inventions: the gate at my aunt's farm and the Squeeze Machine. I just made them. No plans, no blueprint, no design notes. I think I felt comfortable just jumping in because of being a visual thinker, but also because I was a kid and didn't really know that you should start with a plan.

The first time I encountered architectural floor plans was at Swift and Company. I was working on my Master's in animal science and had spent years studying animal behavior but couldn't read a blueprint. They had given me a highly detailed layout drawing of the entire plant and the grounds it was built on. As I walked around, it became obvious that a big round circle on the drawing was the water tower. Other details on the drawing were less obvious, such as extra lines drawn in a wall to show where a window was located or how a square on the floor plan corresponded to a concrete support column that held up the roof. To learn, I had to take the set of drawings for an existing building and literally walk around in the structure with the drawing.

I'm sure I must have looked pretty strange going around and around that plant, but after two days, I was able to relate every line on the drawing to both the structure of the building and the equipment in it. After that, everything started to make sense. To further learn how the drawing related to the structure, I went out to the feedlots and measured existing cattle-handling facilities. Then I used the measurements to make a first draft of a drawing. To check it for accuracy, I went back out to the feedlot and walked around to determine that my drawing was correct. I didn't just rely on memory. This trained my mind to be able to look at drawings and see the completed structure.

Just for fun, take a piece of paper (graph paper if you have it) and draw the shape of your bedroom. Then add squares and rectangles for all the furniture: bed, desk, bureau. Make sure everything is proportional. Take another sheet of paper and draw the four walls with the doors and windows. This is your floor plan. You can add what are called the "schematics," which are the electrical connections or outlets. Don't forget to include any overhead lighting. If you then pushed the furniture around your room so that it no longer looked like your room, you could give your plans to anyone and they would be able to put it back together. Basically, blueprints are instructions for where things go.

LET THERE BE LIGHT

According to the website Great Black Heroes, Lewis Latimer made instrumental contributions to two monumental inventions we now take for granted: the telephone and the lightbulb. Latimer drafted the drawings used to patent Alexander

Lewis Latimer

Source: Wikimedia Commons

Graham Bell's telephone, and in creating a slow-burning carbon filament, he improved upon Thomas Edison's light-bulb, making it more practical for home use and therefore more widespread.

The son of escaped slaves, Latimer was born in Massachusetts as a free man in 1848. He enlisted for the Union in the Civil War at the age of fifteen and returned to Boston two years later with an honorable discharge. At seventeen, he was hired as an office boy at a patent firm and taught himself drafting by observing others at the company. His talent must have been prodigious because he was recognized by the owners and promoted to head draftsman. He went from earning $3 a week to $20 a week in just seven years at the age of twenty-five.

Latimer was granted his first patent in 1874 for an improved water closet (bathroom) on trains. He also held patents for an early air conditioning and sanitizing system, a locking rack for hats and coats, a safety feature for elevators, and the filament to Edison's lightbulbs. In a 1988 *New York Times* article, "A Campaign to Remember an Inventor," Latimer was also credited with the installation of electrical lights in the streets and buildings of major cities such as New York City, Philadelphia, Montreal, and London. He helped illuminate our lives inside and out.

▷ ▷ ▷

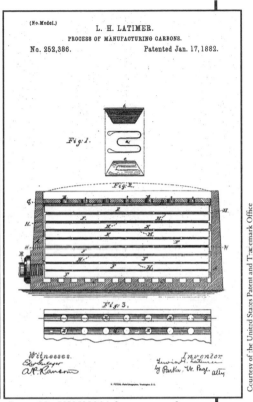

Patent No. US255212A for a globe supporter for electric lamps by John Tregoning and Lewis H. Latimer

Patent No. US252386A for a process of manufacturing carbons by Lewis H. Latimer

My early drawings were crude because I did not know how to use drafting tools. To learn, I watched a talented draftsman named Davy Jones. I studied how he drew a pipe to look 3-D, or how he drew dots and texture to show a concrete slab. Learning to read drawings took time, but once I did, producing really nice drawings of new structures was relatively easy for me. I bought the same pencil and tools that Davy used, and I started by pretending that I was Davy.

Drafting is considered a "universal language" because blueprints can be understood by any builder, engineer, architect, or

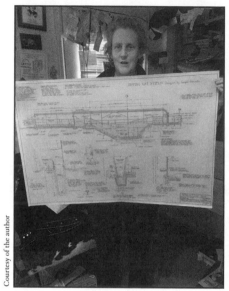

Courtesy of the author

I drafted the schematics for an invention of mine (the dipping vat) with a better entrance design

designer. As we have seen in all the beautiful patents over the past three centuries, it is critical to be able to render your invention as a mechanical drawing. This is how people understand how to make and manufacture it. My very first drawing after I learned to use drafting tools was of a truck-loading ramp for cattle. (It is shown on page 40.) I did all my drawings by hand just using basic tools: drawing board, protractor, ruler, compass, T squares, and a lot of erasers. Now, and pretty much since the nineties, most drafting is done on computers. Of course, there are many ways computers improve drafting, but it's still really important to know how to draw if you want your stuff to get made.

During my career, I learned that it wasn't enough to be a visual thinker if I couldn't communicate my ideas in drawings. I still keep all my original drawings in a flat file in my home in case I need to refer to them or share them with a colleague. I also keep them for another reason: they tell the story of how I became an inventor and found my calling.

· EPILOGUE ·

THE SQUEEZE MACHINE

When I was growing up, people thought that autism was psychological. Physicians had no idea that there were biological components at work, including sensory sensitivities. I used to wrap myself in blankets and get under the cushions of our sofa because of my sensory oversensitivity. My mother saw this as weird behavior. She had no idea how much I craved the pressure of being held. But for many autistic people, like myself, hugs from other people are too jarring to our nervous systems, which is why we pull away. This behavior was also seen as strange. I used to dream of a machine that could hold me tightly, a box with a liner that would inflate.

I saw the machine I dreamed of at my aunt Ann's ranch, only it was used for holding or restraining cattle when they needed their vaccines. The pressure applied to both sides of the animal relaxed it. I was nervous about asking my aunt if I could try it. I cared about what she thought of me, so I gave her a handwritten note. She read it, and we went right out to the squeeze chute. When I got inside, the pressure instantly calmed my anxiety. The effect lasted for about one hour. It was the first time I felt truly like myself.

My original model for my Squeeze Machine

When I got back to my high school, a big panic attack motivated me to build a calming machine for myself. I used old discarded side boards from a pickup truck that was owned by a construction worker. My experience making things helped me to build my first machine, which I did without a blueprint or plan. If could see it in my mind, I could build it. The design was in my imagination and not on a drawing. Unfortunately, the headmaster and psychologist at the school thought it was weird and maybe dangerous. They called my mother, and they wanted me to get rid of it. No one understood how much I needed the pressure to relax my overactive nervous system except Mr. Carlock, my high school science teacher. He invited me into his shop to work on it and challenged me to build a better machine, which I nicknamed the Squeeze Machine. Being able to work with Mr. Carlock throughout high school helped me to make the transition to college. In science and life, I can't overstate the need for mentors, guides, and teachers.

Mr. Carlock also encouraged me to publish my findings in a study. Many years later, I submitted the results in an article for the *Journal of Child and Adolescent Psychopharmacology* called "Calming Effects of Deep Touch Pressure in Patients with Autistic Disorder, College Students, and Animals," which is a fancy way of explaining how the Squeeze Machine works. All throughout my life, I've written papers and articles to record the work I've done with cattle, construction, animal behavior, and autism. I encourage all my students to do so. Think of it as an intellectual patent, a place to store your knowledge. Writing papers did not come easily to me, but once I learned the main features of a journal article—once I could picture them—I could do it. The steps are:

1. First read the magazines where you want to publish your work. Get a feel for the articles that interest them and the general length. If they run five-hundred-word stories, don't submit a two-thousand-word story.

2. Ideas. I got them out in the field. One of my stories was about a new dairy that was being built. Another was about these huge Charlais bulls that were being imported from France for the first time.

3. Structure your article: introduction, body, conclusion. It helps to sketch out your ideas on index cards first. This way you can organize your thoughts and the story's components.

After I graduated from Franklin Pierce College, I constructed a third and final version of the Squeeze Machine. As I built it, I figured out ways to improve it. All the inventing was done in the shop, where I could change the design as construction progressed. Later in my career, I had to do all my inventing on the page. In my imagination, I built three-dimensional steel and concrete structures while drawing. I called this "transferring the shop" from the physical world to the paper world. Learning to do this was essential because it made it possible for somebody else to build my design.

I thought about getting a patent for the Squeeze Machine. I discussed it with Mr. Carlock, who explained that my Squeeze Machine was a new use for an existing device for holding cattle, and that you couldn't get a patent for a new use of something that already exists. The U.S. Patent Office claims that "a new function or unknown property which is inherently present in the prior art does not necessarily make the claim patentable." In the late 1960s, when Mr. Carlock was advising me, this statement was interpreted very broadly. Today it is interpreted more narrowly. If I had invented the Squeeze Machine today, it probably could have been patented. Later, the Supreme Court went on to rule that abstract ideas and natural processes are not patentable. The other component that cannot be patented is something called "know-how," also known as "trade secrets." When you submit a patent, you need to provide every piece of information necessary to build the machine or device, but you're not obligated to divulge *how* to build it or all the little secrets or shortcuts you devised to make it work, more officially known as "proprietary manufacturing procedures." In other words, the patent office gets to pick your invention, but it can't pick your brain.

What makes me very happy is seeing my work cited in other patents. There are at least twenty-three patents that refer to my work for deep pressure methods for autism therapy, as well as for pressure-applying animal garments. I don't need a patent to know that I figured out how to get relief from the terrible panic and stress I felt all the time. Or that I went on to create systems that eased the suffering of animals. In both cases, I observed a situation that needed to be fixed. In both cases, I could see in my mind how to do that. Then I learned how to draft and communicate my ideas. And that, as far as I can tell, is the soul of invention.

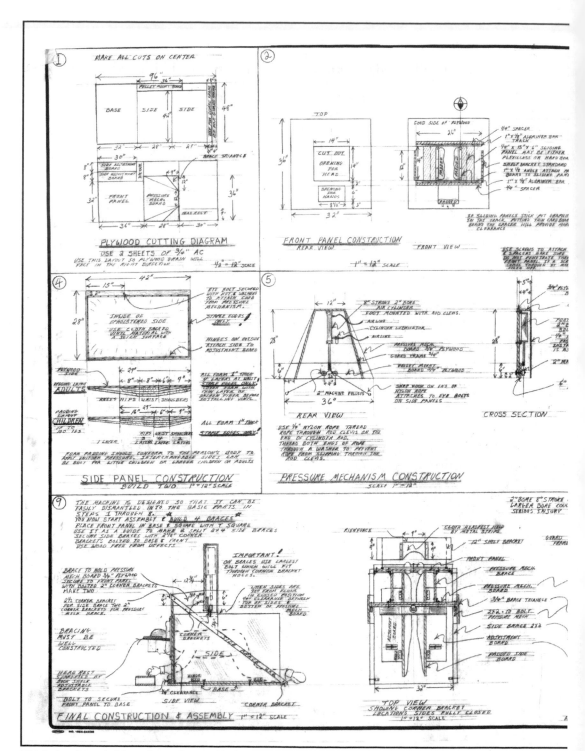

This is the schematic I drew for my Squeeze Machine.

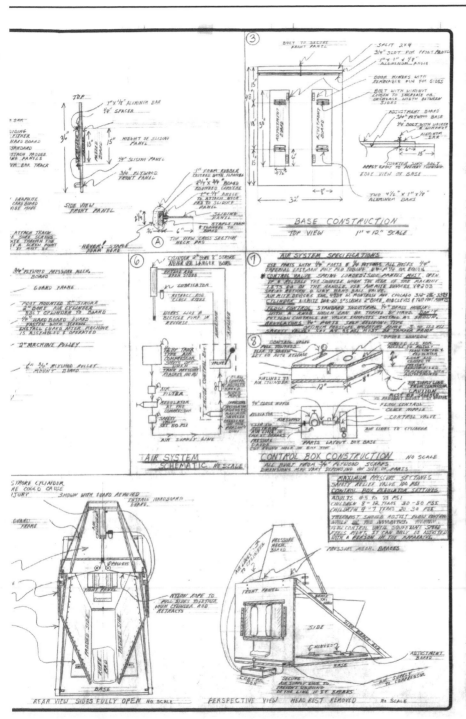

ACKNOWLEDGMENTS

I would like to thank the following people for help with this project: My editor Jill Santopolo, assistant editor Talia Benamy, interior designer Ellice Lee, jacket designer Lindsey Andrews, publisher Michael Green, copy editor Chandra Wohleber, proofreader Elizabeth Lunn, and Jen Loja and the rest of the team at Penguin Young Readers. Special thanks to Cheryl Miller.

BIBLIOGRAPHY

AMES, ADELBERT, JR. *The Morning Notes of Adelbert Ames, Jr.* New Brunswick, NJ: Rutgers University Press, 1960.

ASTAIZA, RANDY, AND KEVEN LORIA. "15 Amazing Science Discoveries Inspired by Complete Accidents," *Business Insider*, June 7, 2014, http://www.businessinsider.com/accidental-science-discoveries.

BALTIMORE LITERARY HERITAGE PROJECT. "Otto Merganthaler, May 10, 1854–October 28, 1899," http://baltimoreauthors.ubalt.edu/writers/ottomergenthaler.htm.

BEHRENS, R. "The Life and Unusual Ideas of Adelbert Ames, Jr.," *Leonardo*, vol. 20, no. 3 (1987), pp. 273–279.

BELLIS, MARY. "Colors of Innovation: History of African American Inventors," *ThoughtCo.*, June 30, 2015, http://www.thoughtco.com/colors-of-innovation-1991281.

BLACKPAST.ORG.

BRODIE, FAWN M. *Thomas Jefferson: An Intimate History.* New York: W. W. Norton & Co., Inc., 1974.

CARLISLE, RODNEY. *"Scientific American" Inventions and Discoveries: All the Milestones in Ingenuity from the Discovery of Fire to the Invention of the Microwave Oven*. Hoboken, NJ: John Wiley & Sons, 2004.

CHAFKIN, MAX. "Virtual Boys," *Vanity Fair*, October 2015.

CHAMBERLAIN, GAIUS. "Lewis Latimer," *Great Black Heroes*, November 25, 2011, http://www.greatblackheroes.com/science/lewis-latimer/.

CHAMBERLAIN, GAIUS. "Lewis Latimer," *The Black Inventor*, March 23, 2012, http://blackinventor.com/lewis-latimer/.

CHEMICAL HERITAGE FOUNDATION. "Stephanie L. Kwolek," July 29, 2015, https://www.chemheritage.org/historical-profile/stephanie-l-kwolek.

COLE, DAVID J., EVE BROWNING, AND FRED E. H. SCHROEDER. *Encyclopedia of Modern Everyday Inventions*. Westport, CT: Greenwood Press, 2003.

DE CAMP, L. SPRAGUE. *The Heroic Age of American Invention: 32 Men Who Made the Modern American Era*. Garden City and New York: Doubleday, 1961.

DE CAMP, L. SPRAGUE, AND CATHERINE C. DE CAMP. *The Story of Science in America*. New York: Charles Scribner's Sons, 1967.

DENHOED, ANDREA. "The Making of the American Museum of Natural History's Wildlife Dioramas," *The New Yorker*, February 15, 2016, http://www.newyorker.com/culture/photo-booth /the-making-of-the-american-museum-of-natural-historys-wildlife-dioramas.

ETHELL, JEFFREY L. *Frontiers of Flight*. Washington, DC: Smithsonian Books, 1992.

FELDMAN, ANTHONY, AND PETER FORD. *Scientists and Inventors: The People Who Made Technology from the Earliest Times to Today*. New York: Facts on File, 1979.

FENSTER, JULIE M. *The Spirit of Invention: The Story of the Thinkers, Creators, and Dreamers Who Formed Our Nation*. New York: Smithsonian Books, 2009.

FRIED, JOSEPH P. "A Campaign to Remember an Inventor," *The New York Times*, August 6, 1988.

GIRDERS AND GEARS. "A Brief History of A. C. Gilbert," http://www.girdersandgears.com/erector-history.html.

GLADWELL, MALCOLM. "The Televisionary: Big Business and the Myth of the Lone Inventor," *The New Yorker*, May 27, 2002.

GOODYEAR CORPORATE. "Goodyear's Beginnings," https://corporate.goodyear.com/en-US/about/history/beginnings.html.

GRANDIN, TEMPLE. "Double Rail Restrainer Conveyor for Livestock Handling," *Journal of Agricultural Engineering Research*, Vol. 41 (1988), pp. 327–338.

GRANDIN, TEMPLE. *Thinking in Pictures, Expanded Edition*. New York: Vintage Press, 2006.

GRAY, CHARLOTTE. *Reluctant Genius: Alexander Graham Bell and the Passion for Invention*. New York: Arcade Publishing, 2006.

THE HARRY RANSOM CENTER AT THE UNIVERSITY OF TEXAS AT AUSTIN. "Gutenberg's Legacy," http://www.hrc.utexas.edu/educator/modules /gutenberg/books/legacy/.

HOWARD, FRED. *Wilbur and Orville: A Biography of the Wright Brothers*. New York: Alfred A. Knopf, 1987.

HYLANDER, C. J. *American Inventors*. New York: The MacMillan Company, 1955.

ISAACSON, WALTER. *Einstein: His Life and Times*. New York: Simon & Schuster, 2007.

JEFFERSON'S MONTICELLO. "Patents," https://www.monticello.org/site/research-and-collections/patents.

KEENAN, BILL. "Reverend Paterson Invents the Gutta Percha Ball 1848," http://lorespot.com/lore-moment/2013/2/25 /reveren-paterson-invents-the-gutta-percha-ball-1848.

KUSHNER, DAVID. "Will Virtual Reality Change Your Life?," *Rolling Stone*, June 2, 2016.

LAFRANCE, ADREINNE. "Why Do Women Inventors Hold So Few Patents?," *The Atlantic*, July 21, 2016.

LAMMIE, ROB. "Whiz Kids: 5 Amazing Young Inventors," http://mentalfloss.com/article/28546/whiz-kids-5-amazing-young-inventors.

LIBBRECHT, KENNETH G. *The Little Book of Snowflakes*. Minneapolis: Voyageur Press, 2004.

MACARTHUR, PAUL J. "The Top Ten Important Moments in Snowboarding History," Smithsonian.com, February 5, 2010, https://www.smithsonianmag.com/history/the-top-ten-important-moments-in-snowboarding-history-6851590.

MUIR, HAZEL. "Einstein and Newton Showed Signs of Autism," *The New Scientist*, September 30, 2017, https://www.newscientist.com/article/dn3676-einstein-and-newton-showed-signs-of-autism/.

MUSEUM OF AMERICAN HERITAGE. "Stitches in Time—100 Years of Machines and Sewing," http://www.moah.org/stitches/index.html.

NASA. "Aviation Pioneer Richard T. Whitcomb," http://www.nasa.gov/topics/people/features/richard_whitcomb.html.

NEBRASKA STATE HISTORICAL SOCIETY. "Homan J. Walsh and the Kite That Helped Build a Bridge," May 2010, http://www.nebraskahistory.org/publish/publicat/timeline/kite_bridge.htm.

THE NEW YORK TIMES. "Presidential Perspectives: Biography of Shirley Ann Jackson, PhD," 2004, http://www.nytimes.com/ref/college/faculty/coll_pres_jacksonbio.html.

NOE, RAIN. "A Brief History of Golf Ball Design and Why You Shouldn't Hit People with Baseball Bats," Core 77, July 19, 2013,

http://www.core77.com/posts/25240/A-Brief-History-of-Golf-Ball-Design-and
-Why-You-Shouldn't-Hit-People-with-Baseball-Bats.

O'CONNOR, J. J., AND E. F. ROBERTSON. "Leonardo Pisano Fibonacci,"
MacTutor History of Mathematics Archive,
http://www-history.mcs.st-andrews.ac.uk/Biographies/Fibonacci.html.

PAPER INDUSTRY HALL OF FAME. "Louis-Nicolas Robert," Paper
International Hall of Fame, https://www.paperdiscoverycenter.org/inductees
/louis-nicolas-robert/.

PEARCE, JEREMY. "Stephanie L. Kwolek, Inventor of Kevlar, Is Dead at 90," *The
New York Times*, June 20, 2014.

PTACEK, GREG AND ETHLIE ANN VARE. *Mothers of Invention*. New York,
NY: Quill/William Morrow, 1987.

ROBINSON, M. "The Kite That Bridged a River,"
http://kitehistory.com/Miscellaneous/Homan_Walsh.htm.

SANDEL, DAVID. "A Brief History of Snowboarding," *Liftopia*, December 23,
2014, http://blog.liftopia.com/history-of-snowboarding/.

SCIENTIFIC AMERICAN. "How Do Dimples in Golf Balls Affect Their Flight?,"
September 19, 2009, https://www.scientificamerican.com/article
/how-do-dimples-in-golf-ba/.

SCOTTISHGOLFHISTORY.ORG. "Golf Ball from Hairy to Haskell,"
http://www.scottishgolfhistory.org/origin-of-golf-terms
/golf-ball-feathery-gutty-haskell/

SHAW, JONATHAN. "Who Built the Pyramids?," *Harvard Magazine*,
July–August 2003, http://harvardmagazine.com/2003/07
/who-built-the-pyramids-html.

SOMMA, ANN MARIE. "Charles Goodyear and the Vulcanization of Rubber,"
http://connecticuthistory.org/charles-goodyear-and-the-vulcanization-of-rubber/.

STANLEY, AUTUMN. *Mothers and Daughters of Invention*. New Brunswick, NJ: Rutgers University Press, 1993.

SWEARINGEN, JAKE. "An Idea That Stuck: How George de Mestral Invented the Velcro Fastener," The Vindicated, *New York Magazine*, November 1, 2016, http://nymag.com/vindicated/2016/11/an-idea-that-stuck-how-george-de-mestral -invented-velcro.html.

TEMPLE UNIVERSITY. "The Fibonacci Sequence, Spirals and the Golden Mean," https://math.temple.edu/~reich/Fib/fibo.html.

TUNNICLIFFE, SUE DALE, AND ANNETTE SCHEERSOI. *Natural History Dioramas: History, Construction and Educational Role*. New York: Springer, 2014.

UNITED STATES NATIONAL LIBRARY OF MEDICINE. "Changing the Face of Medicine: Patricia E. Bath," October 14, 2003, https://cfmedicine.nlm.nih.gov/physicians/biography_26.html.

UNITED STATES PATENT AND TRADEMARK OFFICE. "General Information Concerning Patents," https://www.uspto.gov /patents-getting-started/general-information-concerning-patents.

WALKER, JOHN R., AND BERNARD D. MATHIS. *Exploring Drafting: Fundamentals of Drafting Technology*. Tinley Park, IL: The Goodheart Willcox Company, Inc., 2007.

INDEX

NOTE TO READERS: Entries listed here in bold refer to projects.
Page numbers listed in italics indicate photos or illustrations.